UFOS

UFOS

by Dr. Virigina Bennett

Illustrated by Bill McDonald

Ronin Publishing

Berkeley, CA

UFOs
ISBN: 1-57951-057-4
Copyright © 2003 by Ronin Publishing, Inc.

Published by
RONIN Publishing, Inc.
PO Box 22900
Oakland, CA 94609
www.roninpub.com

Credits:

Editor:	**Beverly A. Potter**	www.docpotter.com
Cover Design:	**Generic Type**	www.generictype.com
Illustrations:	**Bill MacDonald**	www.AlienUFOart.com

Distributed to the trade by **Publishers Group West**
Printed in the United States of America by **Arvato**

Library of Congress Card Number: 2002096224
Printing Number 1

ACKNOWLEDGEMENTS

I WISH TO THANK Nancy Talbott of the BLT Research Team and Ruben Uriarte, Director of Northern California MUFON for invaluable information, assistance, and photographs. Special appreciation goes to Michael Miley of *UFO Magazine* for talking through the perplexities of ufology, Julian for the "down-to-earth" perspectives on astrophysics, and to Bob and Teri Brown for their International UFO Congresses that have rocked my world. Extra thanks goes to Bill—for being Bill—to Beverly Potter, Ronin's |publisher, for giving this book life and form, and to Bill McDonald for his amazing art images based on real alien/UFO abduction cases. As always, I am indebted to my clients, who are my real teachers.

Credits

Design and developmental editing by Beverly A. Potter, www.docpotter.com

Cover design by Generic Typo, www.generictype.com

Fonts: Aerospace by Bitstream

Gouty Old Style by URW

SFZero Gravity by Shy Fonts

Spumoni LP by LetterPerfect Design

Photographs of alien autopsy were found at A Truely Dangerous Company (www.trudang.com/autopsy/howto1.html) and originated from *Alien Autopsy*, movie by Santilli.

Photographs of grain taken from inside crop circles and of mutulated cattle are reprinted by permission of Namcy Talbot, BLT Research Team, POB 40127, Cambridge, MA. Phone: 617/492-0415, Email: bltresearch@attbi.com, www.bltresearch.com

Alien art images were created by William L. McDonald, AlienUFOart.com

Photographs of crop circles were taken by Rubin Urarte

Illustations of chupracabra were reprinted from *Evidencia OVNI*, Puerto Rico, by permission of Jorge Martin, Publisher.

Clipart is from Hemera Technologies, www.hemera.com

Photographs of Roswell crash debris, dummies and weather balloons were provided by the US Government Printing Office.

TABLE OF CONTENTS

TABLE OF CONTENTS CONTINUED

Preface

BY MICHAEL MILEY

UFO MAGAZINE

THE UFO—AND THE EXTRATERRESTRIAL INTELLIGENCE IMPLIED whenever anyone says *unidentified flying object*—is one of the greatest mysteries of modern times. Elusive, shape-shifting, always just beyond our reach or comprehension, the UFO represents a horizon of possibility that threatens to affect everything we think we know about ourselves, the Earth, the Cosmos, even the Spirit. Anyone who's looked long and hard at the topic knows what I'm talking about—since they'll have progressed beyond the tabloid nonsense peddled by the media or the knee-jerk dismissals of most scientists and academics who haven't really bothered to examine the data. They'll know that the UFO phenomenon is profound and unsettling. Why? Because it shows a *great power*, largely hidden from us. Because it implies a *superior* and *alien* intelligence. And because it defies our attempts at understanding it, often behaving as if it were simply *toying* with us or *deceiving* us, both as to its reasons for being here, as well as to its motives for doing what it does.

Since Antiquity

For starters, UFOs may not be a modern phenomenon at all. As Dr. Virginia Bennett notes early on in her book, there's evidence that UFO encounters can be traced to much earlier times. Aboriginal cave paintings, ancient Japanese clay figurines, masks from Yugoslavia circa 4500 BC, carvings on Mayan temples and sarcophagi—all show strange figures that can be construed as extraterrestrials, sometimes with the large heads and slanted, insect-like eyes you hear about so often in contemporary reports. However, for some reason that's not entirely clear, the modern world has seen an explosion of UFO encounters, from multiple sightings both filmed and videoed, to rumors of landings in out-of-the-way places, to the alien abduction phenomenon, which touches us intimately in our homes and in our bodies. Are we a biological engineering project? Is the Earth property? Is our neck of the Cosmos replete with many highly-evolved species now competing for the same resources as we are? And does our interaction with this intelligence involve even the death-rebirth cycle, as some evidence suggests?

Enigma

Dr. Bennett knows from her own experience, from the encounters of her clients as discovered in therapy, and from in-depth scholarly research, that the UFO is an *enigma machine* that throws off these riddles in the form of a strange light. This light illumines, but it also casts shadows. It takes you on a journey, but you don't know where you're going. You have to keep your wits about you as the floor drops out from under you and you suddenly find yourself standing in mid-air, dazed and confused, in a field of stars. Like the riddles of gnomes, the answers to your questions of the *pilot* of the UFO require a kind of decoding and you may not have the right key.

Beginning

ALL JOURNEYS BEGIN SOMEWHERE and Virginia has crafted here a wonderful little introduction to this strange and powerful underworld. You'll find she's a warm and wise companion on the journey. Travel lightly, she says, and don't take any wooden nickels. And if the gnome of the UFO replies in riddles, wrestle with him and perhaps he'll tell you what he knows. But take heed, be humble. Your ability to understand what he says will be in part dependent upon *who it is that you think you are* and *who it is that this* Other *may ultimately be.*

I'm still travelling the labyrinth and the exit door is nowhere to be seen.

—Michael Miley,
Contributing Editor
UFO Magazine

My Adventure

WITH UFOS

MY INTRODUCTION TO UFOs—UNIDENTIFIED FLYING OBJECTS—BEGAN WITH A DREAM. I was sitting in a dentist's chair waiting for my dentist to do a routine procedure when I became aware of my jaw starting to distort and collapse, followed by my whole body—every bone, sinew, and cell—twisting and compressing into itself, sending shock waves through every muscle. The realization came to me that I was metamorphisizing into—a praying mantis! I woke up in a sweat.

I had been recording my dreams daily for 15 years but I'd never before had a dream like this one. Me—a praying mantis! Deeply perplexed, I pursued its meaning by exploring Jungian archetypes, Freudian implications, and Gestalt techniques. I examined my nocturnal transformation inside out and upside down but its significance eluded me.

Five years later I picked up Whitley Streiber's new book, *Communion*, which was promoted as a "non-fiction" account of his encounters with extraterrestrials. As I read of Streiber's interactions with insect-like beings, memories of my dream flooded back and would not leave me alone. I felt compelled to go to a conference on paranormal phenomena where he was speaking hoping to find out more. For starters, I wanted to know if he was for real or just trying to sell books. During his presentation I was impressed with the sincerity he projected and how he seemed genuinely perplexed by what he had experienced.

Afterwards I asked him if he had heard of encounters with praying mantis-type beings. "Of course!" he said. "There are a lot of people I call the 'praying mantis people' because they have encounters with beings that look like that. There are some folks in Arkansas who claim to have seen a human-sized praying mantis in their backyard."

Hooked

I WAS STUNNED. Seeing a UFO swooping down towards me might have had the same effect on me—but I doubt it. I was unprepared to face that the privacy of my own psyche had yielded this full blown connection to bizarre experiences of strangers scattered throughout the world. Of course, I was familiar with Jung's concept of the collective unconscious but this was *personal*—this was *my* dream. Now it was staring back at me from a really *weird* consensus reality. I was hooked!

Even though I had had a life long interest in paranormal phenomena such as past lives, ghosts, out-of-body experiences, and ESP, I viewed UFOs as merely curious tin cans darting around the atmosphere—a kind of Fortean phenomena, like raining frogs, in which I had little interest. But now UFOs radiated an intensely mysterious power that could affect my deepest self—my very soul. Little did I know I was about to embark upon a cosmically guided, crash-training course in ufology.

At the time, I was in the initial stages of establishing a private practice as a hypnotherapist. Amazingly, the first client who walked in the door wanted hypnosis to help sort out strange experiences he felt were related to UFOs—but he wasn't sure how. Remembering that day, I remain in awe of the synchronicity which brought that particular client to me at that particular time. Our ten sessions proved to be a tour de force of UFO experiences from sightings, to close encounters, to abduction, to past lives, to parallel lives and even to future lives.

Since that first client, I've attended UFO conferences; participated in "abduction" groups for those who have had "too close" encounters; talked with researchers, investigators, and "experiencers;" viewed hours of video tapes and film footage of UFOs; examined countless photographs; gone on numerous "skywatches" to call in alien spacecraft; and conducted hundreds of hours of hypnotherapy with people who have had contact with UFOs and their alien occupants.

My conviction in the reality of the phenomenon has grown in my consulting room where I can feel the atmosphere intensify as a client re-experiences UFO contact. Since that startling dream I earned my doctorate in clinical psychology and have worked in mental health clinics with patients who have schizophrenia, bipolar disorders, and other forms of mental illness. People are my business. I know what psychosis looks like, what it feels like to be in a room with someone who is delusional and, by contrast, how different it feels to be with someone talking about real events. It may not always be clear cut but there are clinical signs and a *feel* about someone that gives clues about who is plugged into reality and who isn't—and who is just making it up.

Opening a Door

IN THIS BOOK YOU WILL BE INTRODUCED TO SIGHTINGS, *very* close encounters, government cover-ups, animal mutilations, other wierd UFO-related phenomena, and theories about UFOs. I will share with you how I came to understand that *something* is going on even if only a fraction of the cases reported are real—and my increasing suspicion the U.S. government is covering up *something*—which supports the idea that there is something worth hiding. The scary question that arises is: If UFOs are real, who is operating them and—most importantly—why?

I've written this book as a guide for newcomers in finding their way to the important landmarks without getting lost in the labyrinth of hoaxes and personal agendas. This is not an exhaustive account of UFOs—nor is it "the Truth." In fact, I caution you to be leery of anyone claiming to know the truth. If ufology teaches us anything it is that truth is relative, contextual, and transitory. When it comes to UFO reports be discriminating, discerning, and even skeptical. Turn your bull detector all the way up whilst exploring this field—yet, keep an open mind. Struggling with this contradictory mind set is not easy and probably one reason scientists, politicians, and academicians prefer to simply dismiss the topic.

Participants Only

STUDYING UFOS IS INHERENTLY CONSCIOUSNESS EXPANDING because the usual means of evaluating information are not available. We develop intuition, while keeping common sense. Don't accept what you are told simply because of the credentials of the reporter. An advanced degree, political position or scientific credential, may mean the presenter is well indoctrinated in traditional views or has a hidden agenda. Credentials and education can get in the way of exploring the unexplained.

On the other hand, someone purportedly channeling a lizard-being from Zeta Reticuli shouldn't be taken on blind faith either. Experience is always real and valid to the experiencer—it's how it gets interpreted that's the kicker. Is a UFO encounter viewed as a religious experience? A scientific marvel? A violent assault? Or dismissed as a figment of imagination?

Everything in this book is controversial—yet it is important! If UFOs carrying alien beings are visiting us—and the body of evidence suggests that this is so—then our worldview will never be the same again. But be careful: the field of UFOs is a "participants only" event. You may think you have had no UFO experiences and never will—and you *may* be right. On the other hand, you have found your way to this little book, so.......

May your adventure begin......

The Baffling World

OF UFOS

LIKE MANY CURIOUS SOULS BEFORE ME, I found myself tumbling into the baffling world of UFOs—a twilight zone inhabited by lizard-like creatures in luminous flying saucers, mysterious Men-in-Black, scientists, spies, and ordinary citizens with fear and amazement in their eyes as they tell unbelievable stories. I discovered a dimension where fantasy and hoax shape-shift into hard-edged reality, then disappear with barely a landing trace left behind.

I learned that UFOs have been reported by thousands of credible witnesses, including police, scientists, jet pilots, and astronauts. Even former United States President Jimmy Carter personally sighted an unidentified flying object. Sightings have steadily increased since the 1940s, to over 10,000 sightings a year reported worldwide by the end of the 20th century. I was not alone in my interest—over 50 percent of the population believes in the existence of UFOs.

The United States government officially closed its last UFO investigation in 1969. Even so, there is increasing evidence that vital information has been concealed from the public. The study of UFOs, known as "ufology," is subject to censorship, fraud, and misinformation, nonetheless the amount of legitimate data is extensive and cannot be dismissed as science fiction. Whatever UFOs are, they are not going away.

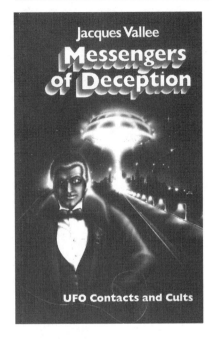

Jacques Vallee
Messengers of Deception

UFO Contacts and Cults

Scientific View

THE SCIENTIFIC COMMUNITY GENERALLY VIEWS UFOS AS NON-EXISTANT or not worthy of serious inquiry. French astrophysicist, Jacques Vallee, author of numerous UFO books including *The Messengers of Deception*, tells of having witnessed French astronomers erase a magnetic tape with eleven data points indicating the presence of an unknown flying object recorded by a satellite-tracking team because they were afraid of ridicule if they presented the evidence. What other anomalous data has been destroyed for similar reasons?

A well-funded scientific project called Search for Extraterrestrial Intelligence, or SETI, holds a more enlightened attitude. They sweep sound waves for radio transmissions from space looking for signs of communication. Yet, it is ironic that SETI spends millions listening to radio signals, while alien spacecraft are apparently zipping around the world being captured on home cameras. Regretfully, SETI scientists refuse to even take a look at other evidence.

Reality Isn't

SCIENCE'S GENERAL DENIAL OF THE EXISTENCE OF UFOS IS REMINISCENT OF THE CHURCH'S REFUSAL to look through Copernicus' telescope to see that earth is not the center of the universe. Apparently, it is simply too threatening to even consider that humans are not alone at the top of the food chain—or to ponder, as one bumper sticker puts it: "Reality Isn't".

Flashes From the Past

I WAS FASCINATED TO DISCOVER THAT UFO ENCOUNTERS HAVE BEEN TRACED back to the very infancy of the human race. In dimly lit Australian caves, for example, aborigines drew human figures wearing helmet-like headgear. Ancient Japanese molded clay figures remarkably similar to contemporary renditions of aliens with strange insect-like heads and eyes, slits for noses, and small openings for mouths. In an Mayan temple, archeologists uncovered an elaborate carving of a helmeted figure curled in a small enclosure resembling a space capsule.

There are references in the Old Testament to UFOs. The Biblical prophet Elijah ascended into heaven in a "chariot of fire." Another prophet Ezekiel described a vehicle in the sky with flames and luminescent wheels. The ancient Hindu text, *Ramayana*, contains descriptions of flying vehicles called "vimana" which were at the beck and call of the gods.

Early Encounters

IN THE NINTH CENTURY, FRENCH VILLAGERS PURPORTEDLY CAPTURED THREE MEN AND A WOMAN as they descended from a huge ship in the sky, claiming they had been taken for a ride in the aerial ship by wise beings who showed them marvelous things. Terrified, the villagers accused them of being black magicians doing the bidding of the malevolent Grimaldus, Duke of Beneventum and stoned the "aerial sailors" to death.

Four centuries later, in an English town, an airship was reported suspended in the sky, with its anchor snagged on a pile of stones. A humanoid who clambered down the rope to free the craft was killed by the crush of townspeople who had rushed in for a closer look.

Flying Cigars

A RASH OF SIGHTINGS OCCURRED IN THE UNITED STATES IN 1896, beginning with bright lights and a cigar-shaped craft over Sacramento, California, followed by other sightings along the West Coast and across the country. Newspaper accounts ranged from "nocturnal lights" to wild tales of two men pedaling large wheels on a flying gondola. One fellow claimed his trousers were caught by the anchor of a craft—a curious detail harkening back to the snagged anchor story from four hundred years earlier.

Flying Saucers

THE TERM "FLYING SAUCER" WAS COINED IN 1947 when a private pilot, Kenneth Arnold, saw bright objects flying in formation, turning and banking at a speed he estimated to be at least 1200 miles per hour. When describing his sighting to reporters he said, "They flew like saucers skipping over the water." He also described them as being like speedboats or the tail of a Chinese kite but it was the image of a saucer that seized the collective imagination. So excessive was the pandemonium from Arnold's account that he later made the statement, "If I saw a ten story building flying through the air I would never say a word about it." ☽

UFOs taunted jet fighters on both sides during World War II and were dubbed "foo fighters"—a play on the French word faux, meaning "pseudo". Both Germans and Americans feared that the strange lights and craft were secret weapons of the enemy.

The Roswell

INCIDENT

THE ROSWELL "INCIDENT" IS THE GRANDDADDY OF CONTEMPORARY UFO SIGHTINGS. Interest in Roswell has made more people aware of the validity of UFOs and the cover-up tactics of the US government than all other UFO reports combined.

New Mexico in the 1940s was the birthplace of the atom bomb and the home to the world's most advanced military installations. The first airborne nuclear weapons were housed in Roswell, a small town nestled next to the 509th Bomb Group of the Eighth Air Force. In July of 1947, a large glowing object was seen speeding through the sky and landing about 75 miles outside of Roswell, near Corona. A rancher named Mac Brazel reported hearing a loud explosion during the night. The next day when he found debris and metallic fragments scattered over a quarter-mile area, he contacted the Sheriff who called in officials from Roswell Army Airfield.

Hieroglyphs

THE AIR FORCE DISPATCHED INTELLIGENCE OFFICERS, MAJOR JESSE MARCEL AND SHERIDAN CAVITT to investigate. Marcel said he found strange, tissue paper-thin pieces of foil-like metal that could not be torn, cut, burned, or in any other way affected or destroyed. There were small strips of debris, half-inch square, light as balsa wood—but so strong they could not be broken or burnt—with hiero-glyphic markings on the sides.

At the order of the base commander, Marcel sent the material to Wright-Patterson Air Force Base in Ohio for analysis. The public information officer, Walter Haut, issued a press release announcing the recovery of a flying saucer, setting off a chain reaction to news reporters from all over the country clamoring for more information.

Back at the Ranch

THE ANNOUNCEMENT WAS SHORT-LIVED. By the time the plane carrying the mysterious debris touched down in Ft. Worth, Texas en route to Ohio, Marcel had been ordered to keep quiet. General Ramey announced that the whole thing was a "mistake." The UFO was actually a wether balloon. To bolster the story Marcel posed with weather ballon-looking debris for the press. The case was officially closed.

After being detained for five days by the military, Brazel was permitted to give reporters only a brief statement confirming the weather balloon story. Following his release, Brazel refused to discuss the matter—even with his own family. Judd Roberts, manager of KGFL

Military investigates the crash site of the UFO just outside of Roswell, New Mexico.

radio—where Brazal had been scheduled for an interview—received a call claimed to be from Washington, D.C. and was told, "We understand that you have some information, and we want to assure you that if you release it...your (broadcast) license could be in jeopardy." Several witnesses, including one from the secretary of the Federal Communications Commission, have verified Robert's account.

The many rumors regarding the flying disc became a reality yesterday when the intelligence office of the 509th Bomb Group of the Eighth Air Force, Roswell Army Air Field was fortunate enough to gain possession of a disc through the cooperation of one of the local ranchers and the sheriff's office of Chaves County. The flying object landed on a ranch near Roswell sometime last week ....

Roswell Daily Record
July 8, 1947

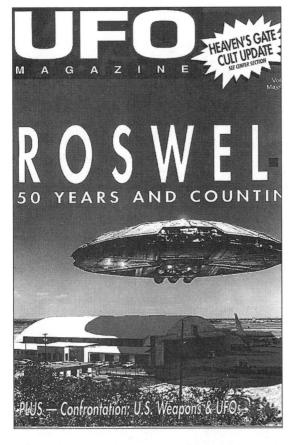

Interest in Roswell Re-ignited

THE INCIDENT WAS SHRUGGED OFF and the story lay dormant for thirty years until Stanton Friedman, a nuclear physicist who authored *The Roswell Incident*, interviewed Jesse Marcel about his handling of the wreckage of the craft, which re-ignited interest in the mystery. Marcel said the debris was unlike anything he had ever seen. He recounted how, at the general's orders, he posed with the "less interesting metallic debris," but the press was allowed only close enough to photograph the material and not permitted to touch it. Marcel said that one photo was not staged and showed debris actually collected at the crash site. He confirmed that the authentic material was sent on to Wright-Patterson. Different debris was then substituted and held up by the general and his aides for further photographing by the press, who were now allowed to closely examine it.

Marcel told Friedman how he had shown his eleven-year-old son some of the pieces and, now as an adult, his son still recalls the strange qualities of the fragments. Subsequently, Friedman gathered reports from 240 people who had witnessed something strange related to the incident or who claimed to have known someone who had.

Second Crash

THIRTY-ONE YEARS LATER IN 1978, A STORY SURFACED that around the same time that Brazel had discovered the debris on his ranch Barney Barnett, a civil engineer with the Soil Conservation Service in New Mexico, had seen a crashed saucer with four alien bodies scattered near it on the Plains of San Agustin.

Stanton Friedman

Barnett said that as he stood there dumb struck, he was unexpectedly joined by a small group of anthropologists who happened to be doing research in the area. Moments later armed soldiers appeared and warned them away from the place, saying that it was a matter of national security and to never tell anyone what they had seen.

Different theories accounting for the second crash site abound. Some believe that, for whatever reason, the alien craft disintegrated in the air before crashing 125 miles away, leaving a trail of debris across Brazel's range. Another possibility is that there had been a mid-air collision between two alien spacecraft.

Whatever the explanation, the unfortunate aspect of the second crash site story is that there are no first-hand witnesses still living today. Barnett died years before UFO researchers could interview him and it was his friends, Vern and Jean Maltais, who conveyed the story to Stanton Friedman. Efforts to locate the anthropologists were in vain. Friedman and his co-author Moore extensively interviewed second- and third- hand witnesses and believe that Barnett did, indeed, find something.

Kevin Randle

Bodies of Evidence

KEVIN RANDLE, AN INVESTIGATOR for the Center for UFO Studies and author of two books about the Roswell case, and his collaborator, Don Schmitt, also believe that there was a second crash site—but in a different location from Barnett's. They obtained a sworn affidavit by a soldier stationed at Roswell at the time, alias "MacKenzie," in which he described the impact site of the alien craft. At the base of a cliff were the remains of a craft, about twenty-five feet long, containing three bodies, with two more bodies sprawled outside the craft. They were humanoid, thin and small, about five feet tall, with large heads and enlarged eyes with pupils.

Lieutenant Shirkey, who flew the plane carrying the wreckage from Roswell to Ft. Worth, said a friend who was the mortician in Roswell, reported that the military purchased his entire stock of child-sized caskets and that he actually viewed the alien bodies. Glenn Dennis, another mortician told Friedman that a nurse he knew, who worked at the base, also saw the bodies and a medical technician further confirmed the story.) ● (

The Curious

Alien Autopsy

Stories of alien bodies at Roswell took on new interest when a film surfaced of a 1947 military autopsy—on an alien! Ray Santilli, a British video distributor, claimed to have bought the film in 1995 from an American Army cameraman who said he did the original filming and had made a duplicate copy, which he kept secret for nearly 50 years. It is rumored that Santilli paid a hundred thousand dollars for the film.

Camera-Action!

In this fuzzy, black and white film you see two people encased in white anti-contamination suits moving around the alien's body, their faces obscured by the glass plates in their hoods as they make incisions, extract organs, and remove the black lens over its eyes. They work rather rapidly, with little hesitation. A third figure, wearing a facemask, peers at the proceedings through a large glass window in one of the walls. The film is often out of focus or blocked by the two people performing the autopsy, conveying the impression that documenting the operation is a low priority.

Is this For Real?

Like many others, I had no problem with the notion of a film per se, since witnesses at Roswell had reported seeing the Army making films and taking photographs. However, there is much about this film that challenges its credibility. For one thing, the alien lacks the anorexic appearance so

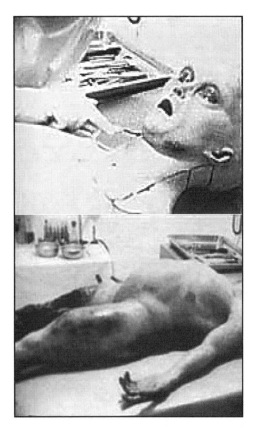

The grainy, black and white film shows a small room with a humanoid body on a makeshift operating table. The head is relatively large with two large dark eyes, ears placed low on the head, a small nose and open, rounded mouth. The being has a large, protruding stomach and somewhat stocky limbs. There is an extensive wound on one of its legs.

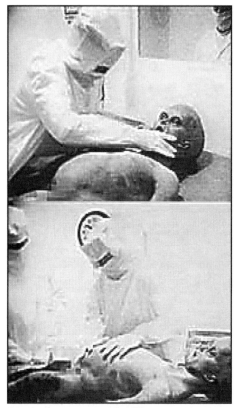

Complete autopsy is in Santilli's movie, *Alien Autopsy*.

often described—the extremely thin arms and legs, flat stomach with holes for a nose, a slit for the mouth and larger, more slanted eyes. Of course, there is no standard for alien appearance, so it would be absurd to challenge it solely on those grounds.

The set up of the room, however, presents problems. The table lacks the channels for fluids found on autopsy tables. Instruments seen in the film, like a palpitation hammer are only used on living bodies and not in autopsies. The doctors convey a disturbingly cavalier attitude towards the autopsy, performing tasks quite quickly, as if they had autopsied hundreds of aliens and knew just what to expect. Only two of the four walls are ever actually filmed, even though the camera roamed, further supporting the idea of a stage set.

Voices of Experience

KENT JEFFRY, A UFO RESEARCHER, INTERVIEWED THREE COMBAT CAMERAMEN involved in classified military projects during the 1940s. Dan McGovern, who had filmed military autopsies, said they used 16 mm color—not black and white—film and followed a standard procedure in which one cameraman operated two movie cameras, one on a tripod and another fastened to the ceiling, while still photographs were taken by a second cameraman. McGovern said the military did not allow cameramen to process the film they shot and all film developed was counted frame by frame to make sure nothing had been taken. Why, at such a historic event as an alien autopsy, standard procedures were set aside has not been answered—which casts a long shadow of doubt over Santilli's film.

Film Analysis

SANTILLI RELUCTANTLY RELINQUISHED A FEW FRAMES OF THE FILM FOR ANALYSIS to authenticate that it was of 1947 vintage. The frames, however, did not include the alien, but only a vague background, which might—or might not—have been the room. The results from analysis were inconclusive. Santilli

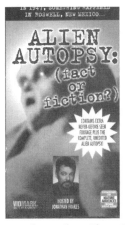

refused to submit frames showing the alien body to Kodak for analysis because, "I simply do not trust an American corporation with lucrative defense contracts."

Cameraman Speaks

THE IDENTITY OF THE CAMERAMAN HAS REMAINED ENIGMATIC. Bob Shell, editor of *Shutterbug* magazine, produced what he said was an "exact transcript" of an audiotape of the cameraman's statement about the film. The terminology was distinctly British in places and unlike language typical of American military personnel. Santilli said his secretary, who transcribed the tape, was British and must have changed the wording. In the transcript the cameraman identified the crash site as just southwest of Socorro, which contradicts earlier reports of it being 200 miles from Roswell. Later Santilli changed his story, saying he did not buy the film from the original cameraman but met him afterwards. Out of the two hours of film Santilli claimed to have in his possession, he presented only twenty minutes for public viewing.

You Be the Judge

SANTILLI'S MOVIE, *ALIEN AUTOPSY*, AIRS PERIODICALLY and is available on video so you can make up your own mind. Some people find the alien looks like a large doll and totally fake, others find it very convincing and realistic. *The UFO Invasion* has a spoof called "How to Make an Alien: A Step-by-Step Handbook" in which they replicated the process they believe hoaxers used to create the alien autopsy. Reality is in the mind of the beholder.

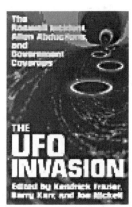

Just

DUMMIES

FRIEDMAN UNCOVERED A FBI MEMO STATING THAT THE WRECKAGE WAS NOT A WEATHER BAL-LOON and was to be flown on to Wright-Patterson. The memo verifies that there would have been little reason to continue the flight of a defunct weather balloon to Ohio or Washington, D.C. Allegations of a government cover-up of the Roswell incident are further substantiated by statements of retired Air Force General Thomas Jefferson Dubose, who was a colonel at Fort Worth at the time of the incident. He reported receiving a call from Three-Star General, Clemence McMillen of the Strategic Air Command in Washington, D.C. who ordered that the wreckage be flown to Washington immediately and to never discuss the matter.

Security Clearance

SENATOR BARRY GOLDWATER VISITED WRIGHT-PATTERSON AIR FORCE BASE IN THE 1960S asking to view the remains of the Roswell crash, which were rumored to be stored there. Even though he was a retired USAF General as well as Chairman of the Senate Intelligence Committee he was denied access on the ground he did not have high enough security clearance. Moreover, Goldwater was admonished to never ask to do so again!

Disclaimers

STILL THERE IS PLENTY OF ROOM FOR SKEPTICISM. For example, Sheridan Cavitt, the Counterintelligence Corps officer who was with Jesse Marcel, holds steadfast to the story that the crashed object was an ordinary weather balloon. Furthermore, not all witnesses who give testimony to UFO researchers can be believed. Stories have a way of changing under scrutiny. For example, Randle found holes in the account of Glenn Dennis, the-mortician-who-knew-the-nurse-who-saw-the-alien-bodies. After exhaustive efforts by Randle and others to locate the nurse, Dennis changed his story about her name and what he knew about her. The mis- and dis-information regarding Roswell has escalated in a circus-like atmosphere and the debate about the existence of a second crash site is especially heated. Most military eyewitnesses remain credible however, and UFO researchers believe an alien spacecraft did, indeed, land near Roswell.

The Right Path

WHEN KEVIN RANDLE CONTACTED EDWIN EASLEY, WHO HAD BEEN THE PROVOST MARSHAL IN 1947, he said he couldn't talk about the crash. Pressing him, Randle asked if the researchers were following the right path by focusing on extraterrestrial origins, Easley responded with: "Let me put it this way, that's not the wrong path."

Randle interviewed Patrick Saunders, an Army Staff Officer stationed at Roswell at the time, who also refused to answer directly. However he wrote, "Here's the truth and I still haven't told anybody anything!" on the first page of Randle's book, *The Truth About the UFO Crash at Roswell.*

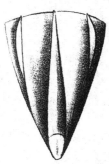

Triangle balloon and drawing.

Military Balloons-Redux

FIFTY YEARS AFTER THE CRASH, the town of Roswell hosted a UFO conference in 1997, attended by 40,000 people, to commemorate the 1947 incident. The Air Force took advantage of the opportunity to give the weather balloon theory another try by releasing a detailed report, *The Roswell Report: Case Closed*, officially stating that what crashed on Brazel's property was a Mogul balloon—a specialized device equipped with carefully engineered acoustic sensors designed to detect Soviet nuclear bomb tests. The Mogul balloon, constructed from rubber, balsa wood, aluminized paper and metal, was larger than the usual weather balloon and had a train of smaller balloons with radar targets attached.

Balloon Theory Thuds

THE MOGUL BALLOON WAS A TOP SECRET PROJECT, which accounts for the tight security around the debris and why it would be flown to another base for analysis. However, a crashed Mogul balloon could not have created that

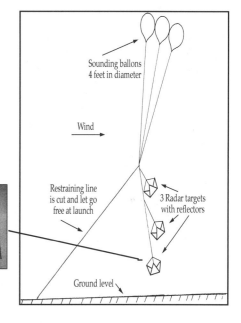

Sounding ballons 4 feet in diameter

Wind

Restraining line is cut and let go free at launch

3 Radar targets with reflectors

Ground level

Airmen with dummy.

amount of debris so how it could have spread over 50 acres remains to be explained. Another contradiction is why the base commander, who would have known about the top security of the Mogul project, would have released to the press a UFO story guaranteed to bring unparalleled public attention.

About the crash Marcel said, "It was not anything from this earth. That, I'm quite sure of. Being in intelligence, I was familiar with all materials used in aircraft and in air travel. This was nothing like this. It could not have been." The Mogul balloon theory leaves us guessing how a well-informed Army officer could mistake rubber, aluminum, and balsa wood as something strange, indestructible, and "not from this earth."

Aliens were Dummies

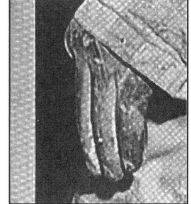

Dummy's hand.

THE AIR FORCE REPORT dismissed reports of alien bodies being found at the site as anthropomorphic dummies. Used to measure environmental effects too hazardous for humans, dummies were routinely dropped with weather balloons throughout New Mexico. These unclassified projects included the assistance of civilians in their recovery.

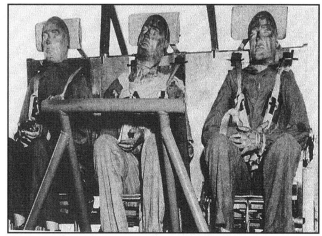

Three dummies ready for flight.

The Air Force reported that the dummies were sometimes transported to and from sites in shipping containers "similar to caskets".

The Air Force photos of the dummies show mannequins, which could, at a distance, be mistaken for alien beings. The report lists quotes from witnesses claiming to have seen alien bodies—the descriptions of which match the characteristics of the dummies. The biggest problem with the "alien-dummy theory" is that *the dummies were not used in New Mexico until 1953—five years after the Roswell crash.* Nor does the theory explain the alien bodies seen at the military hospital near Roswell.

Dummy in a sling.

Time Compression Theory

THE AIR FORCE SWEPT ASIDE THE TIME DISCREPANCY, calling it "time compression" in the minds of witnesses who confused events occurring years apart. According to this theory, the alien bodies witnesses reported seeing at the 1947 crash site were *really* dummies used in experiments with high-altitude parachutes in 1953. The alien bodies seen in a military hospital in 1947 were *really* the bodies of men killed in a crash of a transport plane in 1956.

Case Closed

THE ROSWELL REPORT–CASE CLOSED is the government's official last word on the incident. It hardly dampened the public's fascination with the Roswell crash and actually supports the perception of a government cover-up. The incident at Roswell continues to be a topic of movies, books, and television shows as the investigations—and furor—rages on.

Majestic-12

ROSWELL TURNED "COSMIC WATERGATE" takes on another dimension with the curious appearance of an undeveloped roll of film mailed anonymously to Jaime Shandera who had been working with William Moore, a colleague of Friedman. When developed, the photo showed a nine-page, top secret document addressed to President Eisenhower that listed twelve members of a secret group referred to as Majestic-12—MJ-12—assembled during Truman's administration to investigate the Roswell incident. It was signed by President Truman. The document stated, "four, small humanoid-like beings had apparently ejected from the crash at some point before it exploded" and "fallen to earth about two miles east of the wreckage site. All four were dead and badly decomposed due to action by predators and exposure to the elements."

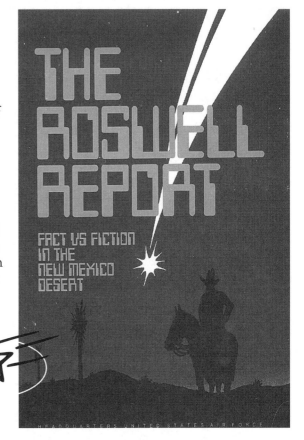

THE ROSWELL REPORT

FACT VS FICTION IN THE NEW MEXICO DESERT

HEADQUARTERS UNITED STATES AIR FORCE

The Air Force advanced the "alien-dummy" theory to explain the alien bodies reportedly seen by witnessess.

According to Moore, shortly before receiving the film, Shandera and he had met with military intelligence agents who intimated they wanted to leak secret information to the public. Shortly after developing the film, an anonymous postcard arrived directing them to documents in the National Archive that had just been declassified. This leak led to the discovery of a memo from Eisenhower's national security advisor, Robert Cutler, to the Chief of Staff of the Air Force, General Nathan Twining, designating a briefing of the "National Security Council MJ-12" and classified "Top Secret, Restricted Security Information."

No Smoking Gun

HERE WAS AN ACTUAL, PHYSICAL DOCUMENT, COMPLETE WITH OFFICIAL WATERMARK that substantiated the existence of MJ–12! The purpose of the group, however, was not stated. The film mailed to Shandera and Moore provided that information but the original document never surfaced—causing heated controversy within the UFO community.

Kevin Randle identified numerous discrepancies with the document and is convinced it is a fake. For example, the second page of the document reads *"Briefing Officer: Adm. Roscoe H. Hillenkoetter (MJ-1)."* However Hillenkoetter's rank is wrong because at the time he was a rear admiral, not an admiral. Furthermore, the date was not written in military format and the classification of "Top Secret Restricted" was never used by the government and "Restricted" was no longer being used in 1954. Since "Top Secret" is a higher category than "Restricted," these terms would not have been combined.

Expert analysis of the typeface indicated that it came from a Smith-Corona P102 used after 1966. Another problem with the document is that Truman always put his signature immediately following, often even touching the last line of text, but in the MJ-12 document the signature is much lower, leaving considerable space under the text.

On the other hand, based on his research, Stanton Friedman found reasons to accept the documents as authentic, including an expert who identified the typewriter as a Remington P4 from the 1940s. Friedman substantiated that the MJ-12 members could have met on the dates in question and the people named as members would have been likely candidates for such a team. This included the initially unlikely prospect of Donald Menzel—a renowned UFO debunker. Friedman discovered he had close and longstanding connections with the National Security Agency and ties to the CIA. Ryan Wood has done extensive work verifying the documents and found, for example, that "Top Secret Restricted" *was* used. Richard Dolan, author of *UFOs and the National Security State*, is a historian who meticulously combed through government documents from the 1940s to the present. He acknowledges the controversy surrounding the MJ-12 documents but has found enough evidence to state that even if these particular documents are not legimate it is safe to conclude that an organization like MJ-12 did exist. ⌒ ∪

Government

COVERUP

THE US GOVERNMENT LAUNCHED A TOP SECRET STUDY IN 1948 OF OVER 200 SIGHTINGS made by credible, trained professionals, mostly Air Force pilots, code named "Project Sign," to ascertain if the unidentified objects were of hostile origin. The final report ruled out natural explanations and concluded the mysterious objects could be extraterrestrial. General Vandenberg, to whom the report was submitted, refused to accept the findings, demanding that all copies be destroyed, and had the report reissued as "inconclusive." Fortunately, one copy of the original report surfaced in the 1970s under the Freedom of Information Act.

Holding a Grudge

UNDER THE PRESSURE OF CONTINUED SIGHTINGS, THE AIR FORCE RELUCTANTLY BEGAN ANOTHER INVESTIGATION, appropriately code-named "Project Grudge," dedicated to finding natural causes for UFO phenomena or, failing that, to discredit witnesses by questioning their credibility, even attacking their mental stability. Despite its best efforts, when the project was terminated, 19 percent of its cases remained unsolved—mysteries that the Air Force simply could not explain away.

To field the continuing onslaught of sighting reports from both military and civilian sources, a central agency, known as "Project Blue Book," was established to maintain the files. When the project was disbanded in 1969, 21 percent of its cases were unsolved.

Whitehouse Fly-Bys

UFOs HAVE YET TO LAND ON THE WHITE HOUSE LAWN but the year the Blue Book Project was born several UFOs were sighted over Washington D.C. Seven slow moving objects were detected by radar in July of 1952 at the National Airport in Washington, D.C. The objects were about fifteen miles away and estimated to be flying between 100 and 300 miles per hour. When Air Force fighter jets were sent to investigate, the radar blips stopped as they entered the area, only to begin again after the jets returned to the base, leaving the UFOs to hover in tight formation until morning. Simultaneously radar controllers at Andrews Air Force Base saw a brilliant orange sphere hovering over the base.

Hide-and-Seek

THE HIDE-AND-SEEK SCENARIO REPEATED ITSELF A WEEK LATER AS JETS SCRAMBLED FOR INTERCEPTION and the UFOs vanished only to reappear as soon as the planes left. A few hours later the objects were still visible and a new team of jets was sent to investigate. One pilot said his plane was surrounded by a circle of large blue and white lights that disappeared before he could respond. The official explanation was that the radar blips and lights were the result of a temperature inversion. Air traffic controller Harry Barnes, who tracked the sightings, disagreed vehemently, saying the weather conditions did not lend to temperature inversions and did not explain why the blips would disappear and reappear in conjunction with jet presence. Project Blue Book recorded the cause of the events as "unknown."

Just Fireflies

FIVE DAYS BEFORE THE MYSTERIOUS FLY-BYS WERE SIGHTED IN WASHINGTON D.C. two commercial pilots reported six glowing reddish objects flying near them. The official explanation, made by debunker Donald Menzel, was that fireflies had become trapped in the windscreen, which the pilots mistook for high speed UFOs doing aerial maneuvers.

Senate Investigation

PUBLIC DISSATISFACTION WITH THE OFFICIAL EXPLANATIONS pressured the Senate into an investigation in 1966. It lasted one hour and twenty minutes. Major Quintanilla, the Director of Project Blue Book, asserted that most UFOs could be explained and that there was no evidence they were extraterrestrial in origin. Satisfied, the Senate investigation committee turned the matter over to an impartial, scientific research team at the University of Colorado, headed by Edward Condon, a prominent physicist. Condon revealed his bias even before the committee convened when he made the public statement, "My attitude right now is that there's nothing to it, but I'm not supposed to reach a conclusion for another year." A memo written by the project coordinator expressed the intention of finding no evidence to support the existence of UFOs. Not surprisingly, the Condon report concluded that UFOs arose from natural causes. Never mentioned was that 30 percent of the cases buried in the report were left unexplained.

Catch-22

The government claims it is no longer investigating UFOs because they do not constitute a threat to national security—yet it will not release any UFO information on the basis that it represents a threat to security.

No Threat

THE AIR FORCE CLAIMED THAT UFOS WERE NOT A THREAT TO NATIONAL SECURITY and further investigation was unwarranted. With a huge sigh of relief, I'm sure, the U.S. government officially ended its involvement in ufology. Unofficially, however, there is increasing evidence that the government is very much in the business of tracking UFOs and has more information than it acknowledges.

Stanton Friedman and other ufologists petitioned the FBI, CIA, and other governmental agencies under the Freedom of Information Act. When the documents were finally handed over, they were heavily censored, with pages of blacked out material, leaving only a few teasing references to UFOs. Friedman contested this censorship in the Federal Court of Appeals, but after a closed conference with government agents, the Court ruled that the information could not be released because it threatened national security.

Full Disclosure Now

A CAMPAIGN TO INSTIGATE CONGRESSIONAL HEARINGS ON UFOS led by Dr. Steven Greer, an emergency room physician, was launched in 2000. Greer formed the Disclosure Project which gathered over 400 first hand witnesses of UFO and ET experiences from government, military and intelligence agencies. The Project's mission is to force the release of information regarding UFOs, including information on advanced energy and propulsion systems based on alien technology. They are also working to ban all space-based weaponry. Greer believes that the best approach for insuring peaceful interactions will be achieved with a diplomatic stance towards contact with UFOs.●

Lazar

IN DREAMLAND

GOVERNMENT CONSPIRACY THEORIES GOT A BOOST IN 1980 when a man called "Dennis" stepped out of the shadows on George Knapp's television series, *UFOs: the Best Evidence.* Young and clean-cut, he said his real name was Bob Lazar and that he had worked for the U.S. government deciphering alien technology. When he was hired by the Office of Naval Intelligence, Lazar said he was told he would be working on an advanced propulsion system and was transported on a bus with blacked out windows to a military installation deep into the Nevada desert known as S-4, near Area 51, known now as "Dreamland." He was taken to a hangar housing a large, metallic disc-shaped craft that he thought was the latest, top-secret technology and felt excited to be included on the project.

After a short while on the job, Lazar was allowed inside the craft and said he was amazed to find the inner dimensions were child-sized, including seats and control panels. The interior molding was formed as a single piece with no seams or bolts. What it was made of, or how it had been constructed, was a mystery.

The engine was even more baffling. Lazar's assignment was to analyze an unprecedented propulsion system in the lower level of the craft. During a briefing he said he was taken to a room where he was left alone to browse through various manuals with strange transparencies and illustrations of a quality different from most photographic reproductions. In one manual Lazar saw pictures of autopsies on aliens. In another, he read a history of the earth from an alien perspective, in which humans were referred to as very unique "containers" which should be carefully preserved to avoid damage.

Lazar said he was threatened with severe consequences if he revealed anything about the secret project—with a gun pointed to his head to make sure he understood the ramifications! This did not, however, deter him from going public with the information. He hoped that a high profile would protect him and implicate the government if anything happened to him.

Truth or Fiction?

CAN BOB LAZAR BE BELIEVED? Lazar underwent four lie detector tests by four different technicians before he appeared on Knapp's TV special. Three technicians concluded he was telling the truth, although they noted a fear reaction, which could be explained by the threats Lazar said he experienced. The fourth technician concluded Lazar was not telling the truth. Another polyographer tested Lazar in 1997 and deemed his responses false regarding Area 51, but truthful when he described the spacecraft.

Checking Lazar's background yielded little. There was no record of his birth, residences, or employment—which Lazar said was an effort by the government to make him a "non-person" to either discredit him or as a prelude to eliminating him. Part of his story was substantiated when Knapp investigated his employment at Los Alamos National Laboratory, where Lazar claimed he worked as a nuclear physicist. While Los Alamos denied that Lazar ever worked there, a telephone directory of employees listed his name—without, however, indicating his job title. Lazar produced a W-2 form from the Office of Naval Intelligence validating his employment with the government. On the other hand, Lazar could not come up with the names of any fellow students or professors he knew while attending Stanford and MIT, so his status as a nuclear physicist remains uncertain. It has been substantiated that he had the expertise to fit a sports car with a jet engine—his claim-to-fame which he says led to his getting the job with Naval Intelligence.

Night Flights

LAZAR REPORTED SEEING other disc-shaped craft in the hangars at the S-4 facility and that he watched night flights of these spacecraft making test runs. Lazar dubbed one craft the "sports model" because of its especially sleek lines and compact size. He sneaked in a few friends into the S-4 area, who later verified having watched the aerial acrobatics of the vehicles. Lazer was eventually caught by guards during one of his nocturnal visits and was dismissed from the project.

Government Disinformation Theories

AS ANOTHER PIECE IN THE COSMIC WATERGATE PUZZLE, Lazar is one of many claiming to have worked for the government and to having had first-hand contact with aliens or alien technology. Different theories have been advanced to account for discrepancies and the lack of verifiable information in cases such as Lazar's in which alleged government agents break the silence and come forth with stories of their experiences.

The theories invariably begin with Agent X or the current government "whistleblower" or "deep-throat" who reports he—it's seldom a "she," by the way—was intimately involved in covert, UFO related governmental projects. In the first scenario Agent X is a covert government agent assigned to spread disinformation because the government has made a quantum leap in its military technology and prefers the cover story of alien involvement to prevent the truth from becoming public knowledge.

In another scenario Agent X is the government's unwitting pawn for disinformation meant to sound so preposterous that mainstream America will scoff at it and ignore stories of alien crafts. In this scenario what Agent X saw was pure theater. Many believe government agents infiltrate UFO organizations to feed them false information to throw them off the track, or to shore up what Stan Friedman calls the "laughter curtain," so that the general public becomes even more convinced that ufologists are a bunch of kooks.

An example was a television special in which a disguised figure of a deep throat-like character—supposedly an agent—revealed highly sensitive information about aliens which the government had held in custody. He expounded upon seeing gray, lizard-looking aliens listening to classical music and eating strawberry ice cream—their favorite treat! For every viewer who may have swallowed this story, there must have been a hundred who dismissed it along with all the other information—some of it legitimate—presented on the show. Many ufologists believe this is exactly the response the government intended.

Covert Release of Information

IN THE FINAL SCENARIO, AGENT X IS PART OF A PLANNED PIECEMEAL DISSEMINATION of real information to the public to accustom us to the reality of aliens. Agent X is credible enough to be believable to many, yet so offbeat that the scientific community, as well as the government, simply ignore him. In this ploy, the government succeeds in sidestepping responsibility to either affirm or deny the existence of aliens among us yet still disseminates information. ❲

Flaps

AND BOGIES

MULTIPLE UFO SIGHTINGS IN A GIVEN AREA IS CALLED A "FLAP." Belgium, is known for flaps with as many as 3,500 sightings reported in a single year. In one incident, UFOs were tracked on four NATO radar systems simultaneously while 300 witnesses spotted a huge, boomerang-shaped craft, the length of a football field, hovering in the skies over Brussels. The president of Belgium publicly acknowledged the sightings to be of unknown origin and cooperated with UFO research teams during their investigations.

Big Bertha

"BIG BERTHA," AS UFO BUFFS AFFECTIONATELY CALL the large, boomerang-shaped crafts, seems to frequent Fyffe, Alabama. The town's sheriff estimates that sightings have occurred weekly for years. Since the 1980s over a hundred witnesses have reported seeing lights, often in triangular formation, crossing the sky. At times the outline of a craft, varying in length from one to three football fields, is visible. The craft, as well as other unexplained lights have been seen hovering several hundred feet above the ground, moving slowly across the sky, then darting suddenly to the horizon at great speed and disappearing.

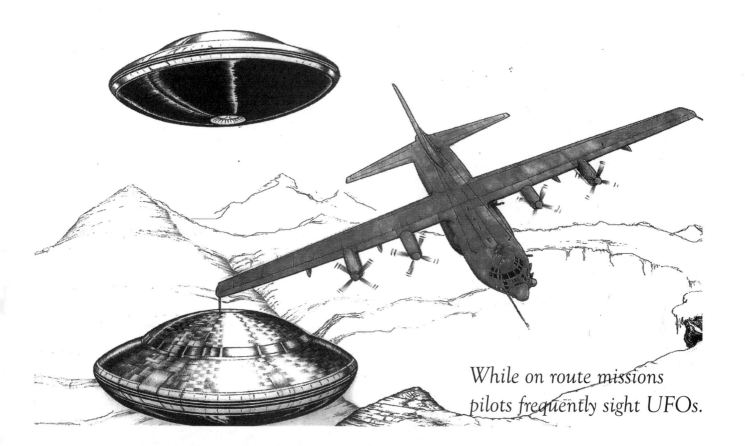

While on route missions pilots frequently sight UFOs.

Night Siege

BIG BERTHA'S TRAIL LEADS BACK TO THE EARLY 1980s to New York's Hudson Valley. *"Hundreds Claim To Have Seen UFOs"* screamed out of the headlines of the Westchester-Rockland Daily Item on March 26, 1983. Yorktown Police Station was flooded with calls on the evening of March 24 from people seeing a boomerang-shaped craft with red, blue, and green lights attached. Witnesses, including police officers, said they saw a multitude of rainbow lights and could see the underside of the craft, which cruised so slowly that one man claimed that he kept up with it while jogging.

By 1987 five thousand sightings had been made in Hudson Valley and neighboring Connecticut counties. The FAA investigated the flight records of all the airports in the Hudson Valley area without finding anything that would account for the UFOs. Stewart International Airport confirmed there had been no commercial or military flights crossing through the area at the time of the sightings. No radar reports were made, but being below 1000 feet, the craft would not have been detected in any case.

Eclipse Sighting

AN ESTIMATED TEN MILLION PEOPLE IN MEXICO WERE LOOKING SKYWARD at 1:15 in the afternoon, in 1991, waiting for a break in the clouds to reveal a total eclipse. As the clouds parted and the sun became a darkened disk, other objects appeared and were filmed by the many video cameras focused on the eclipse. When Jaime Maussan, one of the most popular television personalities in Mexico and host of a show similar to *Sixty Minutes*, asked viewers to send in their videos of these unidentified flying objects, he was besieged with tapes which continued to arrive for more than seven years!

Skeptics claimed that people must have seen Venus or stars, which appeared as the sun darkened. Some of the videos, in fact, showed these—but many showed something more. A video made by the Fuillermo Arreguin, a cameraman for *Televisa*, revealed a craft with sloping sides, an elongated shape and flattened upper and lower surfaces, emitting a dim, violet light from the bottom. Other videos showed an object that looked like an overturned pie pan. On the videos the object remained stationary, then suddenly shifted and moved in a straight line, then again was still. Videos of Venus and stars did not show this behavior.

Office Sightings

IN 1997, IN BOSQUES DE LAS LOMAS, THE WEALTHY SUBURB OF MEXICO CITY, a group of young men in an office caught sight of a large, disc-shaped craft—forty to sixty feet long—rotating and oscillating about a hundred feet in the air, as it slowly moved past the surrounding buildings. The object had a classic UFO shape—an upper dome, elongated curved edges and a flat bottom. One man grabbed a digital video camera and filmed about ninety seconds of the craft's movement until it went behind a building and was not seen again.

Jaime Maussan sent the film to Jim Dilettoso of Village Labs in Tempe, Arizona who had extensive experience in the photo analysis of UFOs. Dilettoso concluded that the film showed no indications of digital manipulation and that the object was not a suspended model. Analysis of the craft's flight pattern indicated it had an independent power source rather than being a radio controlled model or some form of balloon.

Phoenix Lights

SEVEN LIGHTS TRAVELING IN A PERFECT V-FORMATION WERE SEEN BY MULTIPLE WITNESSES crossing the night skies of Phoenix, Arizona in 1997. Other lights and formations were reported, including the outlines of a huge, black triangular craft—over a mile long—flying soundlessly about 30 to 40 miles an hour under the 1200 feet used to detect planes—below radar detection. A home video showed a string of lights stretched across the night canopy hovering in a stationary position before drifting off behind a mountain ridge.

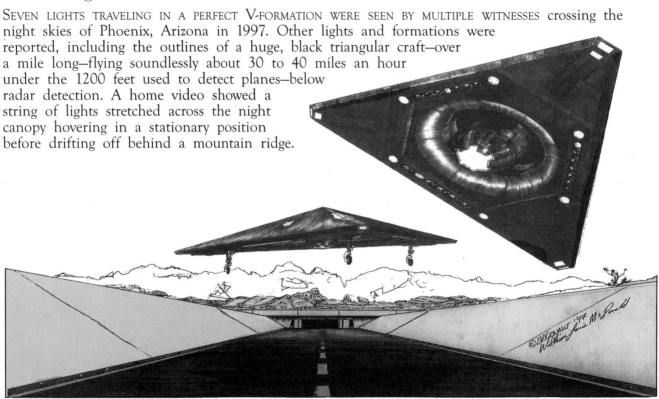

Phoenix City councilperson Frances Barwood expressed legitimate concern about possible unidentified flying aircraft, especially a huge aircraft, cruising over a major metropolis. She launched "Citizens' Right to Know" about UFOs—demanding pertinent government information—as a political platform in her campaign for Secretary General of Arizona—which she lost.

UFOs and Astronauts

ON GEMINI 4, IN 1965, ASTRONAUT JAMES McDIVITT PHOTOGRAPHED A UFO and in a letter to Timothy Goode, author of *Above Top Secret*, described it as "cylindrical in shape. From one end protruded a long, cylindrical pole." Unfortunately, the film was lost or destroyed in transmission down to Houston.

Maurice Chatelain, former Chief of NASA Communications Specialists and involved in designing the Apollo spacecraft, authored *Our Ancestors Come from Outer Space*, in which he says that all of the Apollo and Gemini flights were followed by extraterrestrial spacecraft. Chatelain confirmed reports that Neil Armstrong saw a large spacecraft along the rim of a moon crater.

Astronaut Gordon Cooper publicly stated that he saw UFOs on more than one occasion—although not while on space flights. In 1951, when he piloted a fighter over Germany he and other pilots saw "an armada of flying saucers" streaming in formation past the jets. Cooper said he couldn't catch up to them although he got close enough to discern their saucer shape and metallic surfaces.

Cooper recounted that USAF photographers showed him a film of the landing and take off of a UFO on a dry lakebed in the Mojave Desert. Cooper said it was a "typical inverted lenticular saucer" that put down three landing gears on the desert surface, then lifted up again when the camera crew moved closer.

Spacecraft: Bogey at 10 o'clock high.

Capcom: This is Houston. Say again?

Spacecraft; Said we have a bogey at 10 o'clock high.

Capcom: Gemini 7, is that the booster or is that an actual sighting?

Spacecraft: We have several, looks like debris up here. Actual sighting.

Transcript from Astronaut James Lovell's Gemini 7 flight when a bright object accompanied by shimmering particles, "the bogey," was seen trailing across the sky.

In an interview for *UFO Magazine*, Robert T. Leach asked Cooper if it could have been a weather balloon. Cooper replied, "Weather balloons don't usually land on the lake bed, then take off." Cooper says he is not alone in his sightings of UFOs implying that other astronauts had similar experiences but stayed quiet, fearing the publicity that might result from speaking out. ◐

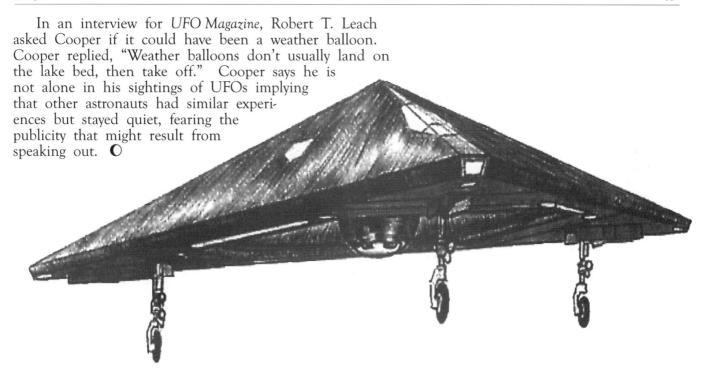

Space Brothers
AND PLEIADIAN VISITORS

IN 1953 GEORGE ADAMSKI'S BOOK, *Flying Saucers Have Landed*, which included photographs of cigar shaped and bell shaped UFO craft taken through his telescope, brought contact with aliens out of the closet and into the public eye. Adamski described meeting a handsome, long-haired, gray-green eyed, human-looking Venusian visitor who landed his craft in the California desert. Using a mixture of broken English and telepathic images the space brother said he had come to "talk" with Adamski and repeated, "Boom! Boom!" meaning the Venusians feared radioactivity from our bombs. He indicated that his spacecraft had crashed on earth and Venusians were killed by Earthlings. He confirmed that Earth humans had been taken away in spacecraft. After their talk he returned to his craft which wobbled as it took off, flashing prismatic colors.

As proof of his amazing encounter, Adamski provided a grainy photo of the craft on a distant hill, plaster casts of the footprints of the Space Brother revealing strange embossed symbols, and a photographic plate that showed an undecipherable written language. Adamski's message to the world was "Let us be friendly and welcome the men from other worlds! *They are already among us.*"

Flying Saucers
Have Landed

Desmond Leslie &
George Adamski

Cosmic Pancakes

THE PRIZE FOR THE ODDEST TALE OF A CLOSE ENCOUNTER GOES TO JOE SIMONTON OF EAGLE RIVER WISCONSIN. Joe, a 60 year old chicken farmer, was home eating breakfast when he saw a rounded silver disc come down into his yard. A door in the craft opened and three beings came out who Joe said, "resembled Italians." They were about five feet tall with dark hair wearing black suits, turtlenecked tops and knitted helmets.

They indicated they wanted something to drink by giving him an empty jug. When Joe returned with water, they were cooking something on a grill without any visible heat source. Being an adventuresome soul, Joe indicated he wanted to try whatever they were cooking. They handed him three pancakes, about three inches in diameter. Joe ate one pancake, which he said tasted "like cardboard" and gave the others to a friend who was a member of the National Investigations Committee on Aerial Phenomena (NICAP).

An analysis by the U.S. Department of Health, Education and Welfare's Food and Drug Laboratory revealed that they contained "hydrogenated oil shortening, starch, wheat bran, soybean hulls and buckwheat hulls." Dr. J. Allen Hynek who investigated the case concluded that Joe had a "waking dream," which he confused with reality. But who's to say what aliens put into their pancakes?

Aliens In Switzerland

HERE IS A UFO CASE THAT I FIND PARTICULARLY FASCINATING. It features hundreds of full color, sharply focused photographs, video tapes and film footage, sound tapes of a UFO craft, and even a metal sample claimed to be from another star system. I met the people involved in the investigation, saw the pictures and listened to the sound tapes of Pleiadian craft—all of which left quite an impression. Yet, the case remains so controversial that many UFO researchers refuse to even discuss it.

It began in a small village in Switzerland in the early 1980s, at the home of a poor, one-armed farmer named Billy Meier. When in a wooded area near his farm, Meier looked up to see a bright metallic disc flying low over the treetops and land in the field where he was standing. Out of the craft emerged a beautiful, Nordic-looking woman who motioned him to come closer. She said her name was Samjase, that she was from the constellation Pleiades and proceeded to tell him about her people and to give information concerning the state of the earth. Samjase met with Meier over the next seven years, establishing telepathic communication to alert him of her arrival and guide him to find the craft. Meier transcribed books delineating Pleiadian philosophy, religious views, and explanations of extraterrestrial travel.

What carries the Meier case beyond similar accounts of people claiming to have had intimate contact with aliens, is the hundreds of photographs Meier took of various Pleiadian spacecraft, including close-range, in focus, color photos along with video and film footage. A top notch special effects artist and model-maker employed by Hollywood film producers said he could not see how the photos could have been hoaxed using a model or other means, "unless Meier had access to a professional studio with $50,000 worth of equipment and a full team of professional assistants."

The Investigation

A TEAM INCLUDING WENDELLE STEVENS, A RETIRED U.S. AIR FORCE COLONEL, AND UFO RESEARCHERS Britt and Lee Elders went to Switzerland for an investigation that took four years. They interviewed Meier and local villagers extensively. Forty witnesses were found who substantiated seeing UFOs, some who had been with Meier at the time, and others who knew of Meier but were not directly associated with him. Witnesses told of hearing unusual buzzing sounds, which Meier claimed originated from the craft. Steven's team collected photographic material, audiotapes of the strange sounds, and even a metal sample which Meier said he was given by Samjase, which they brought back to the United States to be analyzed by independent experts to use in making a video of their findings titled, *Contact: The Billy Meier Case.*

Evidence Analyzed

THE PHOTOGRAPHS WERE SCRUTINIZED BY A PHOTO ANALYST who found no evidence they had been faked in anyway. To fake the shots Meier would have had to have used expensive, cutting-edge photographic technology which did not correspond to the reality of a simple farmer living on a subsistence budget. Further, he would have had to carry models into fields with public access and set them up single-handedly on terrain which did not lend itself easily to such an arrangement, in a small village where neighbors keep a close eye on everyone's comings and goings—especially those of the notorious Mr. Meier, without once being seen in a period of ten years.

One of the 16-mm films showed the craft jumping from one spot in the sky to another *between* frames. There was no explanation for how this could have been faked and not detected by the photo analyst. The sound tapes were given to a prominent audio specialist in Hollywood who handles sound development for leading musicians. He determined that the sounds on the tape were natural, not synthesized and he could not break down the buzzing, whirring sounds into known components. Both he and the photo analysts concluded that if it were a hoax, the person who pulled it off could make a very successful career in Hollywood.

Metal Sample

MOST INTERESTING OF ALL WAS THE METAL SAMPLE THAT WAS ANALYZED BY MARCEL VOGEL, an expert metallurgist employed by IBM. All the metals contained in the sample were found on earth, however, one—thulium, which was first purified during WWII as a by-product of subatomic work—is usually only available in minute quantities at a price that exceeds that of plutonium. The metals were separate and distinct, maintaining their individual characteristics, which perplexed Vogel, who had never seen metals bonded together in this way, and he was at a loss to explain how it could be duplicated. Vogel found grooves at the microscopic level, which seemed to be the result of a machined process. The deeper the levels of the metal, the more intricate the structures became, contrary to ordinary metals which do not reveal these properties. Vogel said it resembled a crystal more than a metallic substance.

Then tragedy struck. Vogel contacted a colleague at NASA to look at the sample. At the meeting Vogel found that the metal sample had disappeared. He had no explanation for how it could have happened. The only evidence that remains is a film of the metal sample made as Vogel performed the analysis, which shows some of the features he described.

Despite the initially positive results of all the analysis, bad luck and controversy have hounded the case. Worldwide publicity inundated Meier with visitors—all wanting a piece of the action. Photographs and negatives were stolen. Some negatives were even burned by Meier's wife in a fit of rage over a phenomenon she did not want to be part of and which was destroying their privacy. For these and other reasons, Billy Meier would not, or could not, give Wendell Stevens the first generation negatives to be analyzed. So despite an overwhelmingly positive indication of the authenticity of the photographs, the analysts refused to give their endorsement without studying the original negatives.

Models Found

RUMORS BEGAN TO FLY WHEN UFO MODELS WERE FOUND in the Meier house. Meier's explanation was that he had made the models years later to compare to the original photos. In fact, photographs, which were made using the models, were easily discernible and did not actually appear until several years later. The analysis of the photos Stevens collected still defied the use of models in their production, but the presence of models on Billy's property was damning evidence that served to close many minds to the case. Most of these skeptics, however, had not done the exhaustive research that the Steven's team had, or even been to Switzerland to understand what the logistics of pulling off such a hoax would entail.

The quality of the audiotapes and the eyewitnesses who confirmed UFOs in the area remain

unchallenged. As the situation in Switzerland became a circus, Meier became reclusive and refused to assist MUFON and APRO, two established U.S. UFO organizations, in their research of his case. Wendell Stevens also refused to send his information to these groups, although he was willing to have them come to him to review the material. Frustrated by what they viewed as a lack of cooperation, the UFO mainstream declared the Meier case a fraud. Meier ultimately stopped having contacts with the Pleiadians, who said that the seven-year cycle for contact had ended, and he is reported to now be withdrawn and unreceptive to visitors. It is rumored, however, that the Pleiadians have renewed contact with Billy Meier. ⌒

Lanterns
AND HELICOPTERS

CONTROVERSY SHROUDS ALL UFO SIGHTINGS. Authentication is invariably difficult and often leads to conflict within the UFO community. Making sense of the photographs which surfaced in the Gulf Breeze incident, is an example. Ed Walter saw a strange glowing object when he looked out the window one evening in 1987. When he went outside to investigate, he saw a spacecraft resembling a round lantern and managed to snap several Polaroid pictures before it drifted away.

Between November 11, 1987 and May 1, 1988 Walters took 39 photographs using five different cameras, including a stereo camera that made it possible to determine the size and distance of the UFO. This camera was provided by the Mutual UFO Network (MUFON) who had loaded, sealed, and taken control shots to prevent trickery. Walters obtained ten UFO photos using this camera.

Walters passed four lie detector tests but photo analysis produced mixed opinions. Dr. Bruce Maccabee, an optic specialist for the Navy, believed the photos were genuine. On the other hand, Dr. Robert Nathan, who worked for NASA's Jet Propulsion Laboratory, was suspicious even though he was unable to prove that they were faked.

Controversy arose when it was found a double exposure could be made with Walter's Polaroid camera. While he denied any knowledge about it, UFO researcher Zan Overall located a Polaroid photo that Walters had taken at a Halloween party showing a faked ghost appearing over the shoulder of one of the guests. It had been created by double exposure.

Walters said that as he ran after the glowing object, a blue light suddenly beamed down from the craft, paralyzed him and lifted him a few feet off the ground. As an intense odor, like ammonia and cinnamon overwhelmed him, telepathic messages told him to calm down. Refusing to obey, Walters yelled in protest and was dropped. The light and the craft disappeared. Walters' pictures were published in the local newspaper, which brought a response from several people who had also seen a craft.

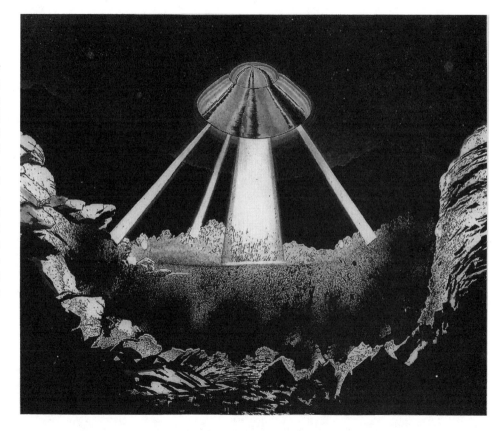

Model Found

WALTERS' INTENTIONS CAME UNDER INTENSE FIRE WHEN AN UFO MODEL WAS FOUND IN HIS HOUSE after he sold it. The miniature UFO was made of Styrofoam and drafting paper covered with sketches of house plans Walters had made. Walters said it was a set-up by debunkers who had stolen the house plans from his trash years earlier. However, the model, it was reported, was not found in plain sight where a debunker would have placed it but behind the attic insulation. If the new owner had not been looking for a water valve, the model would never have been found.

Walters contends the house plans were drawn up for clients two years after his initial UFO photos and maintains that the model does not exactly match the photos. He also bitterly points out that while he underwent four lie-detector tests, his detractors did not have to take any.

Despite the controversy, MUFON recognizes the Walters photographs as legitimate. Whatever the truth about Ed Walters may be, the Gulf Breeze sightings are more than a simple hoax by one man. Lights and crafts were seen by hundreds of people in the Gulf Breeze area. There have been repeated appearances of a red ball of light, which stays stationary for as long as four minutes before disappearing. During one sighting in 1991, thirty-four people were witnesses as MUFON researchers photographed the object, estimating it to be a mile away and about twenty feet across.

The Cash-Landrum Case

UFO SIGHTINGS ARE SOMETIMES ACCOMPANIED BY *IDENTIFIABLE* FLYING OBJECTS—namely menacing, military-looking helicopters. Betty Cash, Vickie Landrum, and Vickie's grandson were driving down a deserted road in Texas one night in 1981 when they saw a blinding light coming towards them. As it got closer they saw that it emanated from a diamond-shaped craft, flames blasting from the underside, which made a beeping sound as it hovered over them. Astonished, they stopped their car and got out to look at it. They said that the heat was so intense that Betty Cash burned her hand on the door handle. As the object gradually moved away, a swarm of twenty large helicopters suddenly appeared and followed it.

Radiation Poisoning

THE NEXT DAY THE TRIO DEVELOPED SYMPTOMS TYPICAL OF RADIATION POISONING, including skin blisters, nausea, and hair loss, and sought medical treatment. The most severely affected was Betty, who had spent the longest time outside the car watching the UFO. The doctors were reluctant to diagnose radiation poisoning since there was no explanation for the source of the exposure—yet there was no other medical explanation. Physical symptoms continued and years later Betty developed cancer.

Removal of Evidence

SEVEN WEEKS AFTER THE INCIDENT, JOHN SCHUESSLER, A UFO INVESTIGATOR, WENT TO THE SCENE and found that the road was blackened and appeared to have been exposed to extreme heat. Shortly afterwards that exact patch of road was dug up by a road construction crew and re-placed.

Betty Cash and Vickie Landrum sued the government, since the sight of the helicopters convinced them of military involvement. The case was substantiated by other witnesses who reported seeing the brilliant light and helicopters identified as Army Chinooks. The Court, however, upheld the testimony of the military and NASA, who claimed they had no such aircraft in the area and the Cash-Landrum case was closed.

More Radiation

TWO OF MY CLIENTS, WHOM I'LL CALL ROSA AND SUSAN, DESCRIBED SIMILAR SYMPTOMS of radiation sickness after a sighting in the Nevada desert. They said that they had sat in a car for two hours watching three huge lights play across the landscape, at times swooping within a few hundred feet of them.

The next day they felt nauseous, lethargic, and had stomach cramps, among other symptoms. Susan said she developed a geometric patter of red blotches on her skin—which had never appeared before or since. Possible UFO radiation exposure is, of course, not the only explanation, but the case is noteworthy because more than one person was involved in both the sighting and symptoms.

The Infamous Men-in-Black

MIB—MEN-IN-BLACK—ARE REPUTED TO MAKE INTIMIDATING VISITS TO WITNESSES AND UFO RESEARCHERS. A typical encounter begins with an expensive, black car driving up, from which emerge one or more humorless-looking men, wearing impeccably tailored black suits. They may wear black hats and dark sunglasses obscuring their eyes. The MIB appear human, yet sometimes speak in stilted or outdated English, like that used in 1940s movies and move in a stiff, robotic fashion. Dr. Herbert Hopkins, who had conducted a hypnotic regression in a UFO case, was approached by such an uninvited visitor whom he described as being very pale, with lips that appeared brightened with lipstick. He was bald with no facial hair, not even eyebrows or eyelashes. After the MIB interviewed the doctor for details of the case, his speech and movements slowed. He said he had to leave because his "energy was running low."

MIB confrontation with aliens

How the MIB know about cases is unknown. Witnesses say that MIBs are fascinated by unremarkable household items, such as ballpoint pens and eating utensils, as if they had never seen them before. MIBs have threatened witnesses, warning them to remain silent. There have been no accounts of actual violence, however. Theories as to who they are range from being federal agents bent on maintaining a government cover-up, to aliens in disguise, attempting to keep a shield of secrecy over their operations, to both! ◖

The Woman

WITH ALIEN EYES

DESPITE MY FASCINATION WITH UFOs, I paid little attention to the "covert government" theories—too paranoid for my taste. Little did I know that an Agent X would be part of my crash training course in ufology until an alien showed up in my living room!

It began when Charlie, a fellow UFO buff, and Ralph Steiner an UFO researcher and investigative reporter for public radio, showed up unexpectedly at my house accompanied by a thirties-something woman, wearing black sunglasses, with blond hair pulled back tightly. She was introduced as "Trixie." As we engaged in small talk, Trixie tensely gripped the chair, her dark glasses still in place, like a celebrity hiding her identity. Eventually, the conversation shifted to the reason for their visit. Trixie needed a place to stay. Before I could respond, she removed her sunglasses with a flourish and peered out at me through dark, alien-looking eyes. The eyes were human-sized but there was no white showing—just opaque, black pools. I experienced a sensation of the floor dropping out from under me, taking my stomach with it. "Oookayyy," I said slowly, "maybe you need to tell me what is going on."

Alien-Hybrid as Houseguest

MY COLLEAGUES LAUNCHED INTO AN INCREDIBLE, CONFUSED TALE OF GOVERNMENT AND ALIEN INTRIGUE. They explained that Trixie had contacted Ralph Steiner because she had heard his radio exposes of government cover-ups of UFOs and alien activity. She had secrets to tell him and needed help with one crisis after another.

Trixie, I was told, had been subjected to all manner of alien interference and U.S. military handling since childhood. In the course of this cosmic abuse, she had developed psychic powers, had been trained by covert military agents to kill, and was abducted repeatedly by aliens. She claimed to be genetically half-human, half-alien—a hybrid who was constantly monitored from an invisible, extraterrestrial spacecraft. Consequently government agents were stalking her, putting her life in danger. She needed a place to hide for a while—an alien safe house of sorts. Could she stay in my home?

I was dumbfounded. The UFO labyrinth had opened its gaping jaws and ensnared me—right in my own home. To say it felt surreal would be an understatement. I tentatively expressed my doubts, saying, "Well,. . . sure, but . . you know . . . I . . . ah . . .I just don't know what can be done with Hollywood special effects. . . ." No, no, no! I was reassured, Steiner and other investigators had taken close-up photographs and examinations the day before and Trixie's eyes were for real. Although they had not had her examined by an opthamologist, they were trying to find one to do so. Charlie slipped me a note as he and Ralph left. It said, "Call me when you get out of here!"

Pistol Packin' Alien

I WAS LEFT ALONE IN MY LIVING ROOM WITH THIS WEIRD ALIEN-HYBRID CREATURE. Gathering my wits I showed Trixie to the guest bedroom where she could stow her few belongings. When I turned to tell her where to find the bathroom I was stunned to see her holding a .38 semi-automatic. Before I could speak, she went out to the back porch and began hitting the pistol against the step to "clear the chamber." While not being familiar with guns, as I watched—from a safe distance—I silently questioned her military training as she fumbled with the gun. Trixie looked dangerous, all right, but not because she had been "trained" to kill.

I took the opportunity to ask—politely—to take a closer look at her eyes and she agreed. With sunlight shimmering through the trees, the unbroken darkness of her eyes stared back at me. I

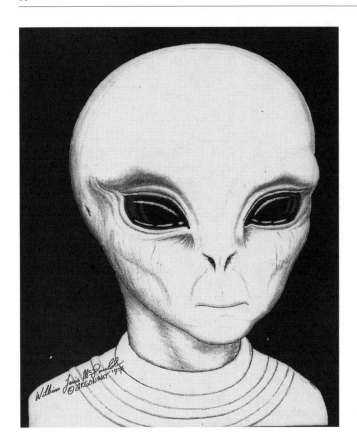

Trixie explained that she was an alien hybrid, that "human eye covers" had been installed so her eyes would appear to be normal. She claimed to have awakened seventy-two hours earlier to find her extraterrestrial brethren had removed her eye covers, exposing her true, alien eyes as startling proof of the truth of her story. She said she was told not to worry because the aliens promised to reinstall the human eye covers—but they didn't say when.

noticed a whisper of an edge around where the pupil would be—but it was too difficult to discern. Trixie quickly turned away and put her dark glasses on, complaining that the light hurt her eyes.

Faked Eyes

I FABRICATED AN EXCUSE TO LEAVE THE HOUSE TO PHONE CHARLIE. Later in a local coffee house as we sipped lattes, he asked my assessment of the situation. "I don't know," I said, "I have an overwhelming feeling that I am watching a scripted drama. Everything she says seems calculated to generate a response. She doesn't seem real to me."

Charlie nodded sagely and told me that the results of the photographic close-up of her eyes showed an opening around the pupil, establishing—without doubt—that she was wearing enlarged contact lenses. As of yet, no one had confronted her or told Ralph who seemed to thoroughly believe her stories and resisted suggestions that she might be a fake.

Aliens Give Back the Eyes

THE CLIMAX CAME THE FOLLOWING EVENING WHEN I RETURNED HOME TO FIND TRIXIE lying on my kitchen floor with the phone in her hand. I slowly walked over to find out what had happened. In a weak voice she said that the aliens beamed her on board their craft, restored her human eyes and dropped her back into my apartment. She had had just enough strength to call Ralph, who was on his way. I noticed that her hair was no longer tightly pulled back and when I asked her about this she said the aliens had washed her hair as well!

Operation Rescue

A GROUP OF US MET INCLUDING, RALPH'S WIFE, TO DISCUSS HOW TO CONFRONT RALPH WITH THE TRUTH about Trixie's eyes being false. This was a rescue operation for Ralph and needed to be handled carefully or he might turn against us and become more embroiled with Trixie and whoever was behind this scheme. Visions of parents kidnapping their own children from the Moonies or other cults flashed through my imagination. Drawing upon my clinical training, I suggested a process in which we each would talk, without judgement or anger, about our own experiences with Trixie and our assessment of what was going on. We hoped that having people Ralph trusted confront him with the truth would awaken him to the reality of Trixie's hoax.

Deprogramming Ralph

A MEETING WAS ARRANGED. Ralph arrived expecting a general discussion of Trixie's plight and how to help her. One-by-one we each expressed our concern and took turns describing what we had observed about Trixie, inconsistencies in her behavior, contradictions in her statements, and the things that just didn't add up.

The kicker, of course, was the pictures. The investigator in Ralph could not deny the visible outline of an opening aound the pupil. For a time he sat stunned and deflated but eventually readjusted to consensus reality. Soon Ralph was actively participating in plans to confront Trixie.

Who was Trixie?

RALPH ARRANGED TO MEET TRIXIE IN A PUBLIC PLACE AND CONFRONTED HER with the truth about the hoax. She denied everything, "I don't know what you're talking about." Further discussion became futile and Ralph left her to fend for herself. A few months later, Trixie went on to deceive another UFO researcher who became so involved that he threatened Ralph when he refused to turn over the tapes of his interviews with Trixie. Where Trixie is now is anyone's guess.

So who, or what was she? The "alien-hybrid" explanation obviously doesn't hold up. Ralph had given her the use of his calling card and the phone records showed she made frequent calls to her husband, from whom she had supposedly "escaped." She also had called Langley Air Force Base, which added to the mystery. Did she really have military affiliations?

Ralph had aired his investigations of alien-related activities on US military bases on the radio. It is conceivable that Trixie was affiliated with a covert government group who deliberately led him on a wild goose chase to make him look foolish and damage his credibility.

Under this hypothesis, it was not essential that Trixie—aka Agent X—actually be believed as long as she created distraction, disunity, and controversy while gathering insider information of what was going on in the UFO community. It has been documented that the FBI and CIA have used similar ploys with groups like the Black Panthers, the Peace Movement, and international political organizations.

Mind Control

RALPH BELIEVES HE WAS THE TARGET of a highly skilled, covert government operative "Mata Hari" who used psychic powers and psychological techniques to destabilize his thinking and emotions. For example, Ralph described talking with Trixie in a college library when a librarian told them to be quiet. As Trixie expressed her annoyance, a nearby copy machine suddenly began dropping coins into the change return—like a slot machine. Trixie lept up and exclaimed, "We've got to get out of here. I can't always stop it once it gets started." The "it" being her psychokinetic powers which had become unleashed by her anger and afflicted the nearest mechanical device—the copy machine. Library staff members told Ralph that the machine had never done this before.

On another occasion Trixie told Ralph she had a severe backache. When they got in his car it wouldn't start. "Oh, no!" worried Trixie, "This happens sometimes," and explained that when she was in pain she could affect mechanical things psychokinetically. After several frustrating attempts to start the car, Trixie got out and the car started easily.

I have a difficult time reconciling Ralph's views, for which I have considerable respect, with my experience of Trixie. I saw her do nothing unusual except consistently behave like a bad actress in a Grade-B sci-fi movie. Perhaps Trixie and her buddies were UFO debunkers who wanted to pull off a grand hoax and humiliate the UFO community along with one of its leading investigators. Maybe they hoped the "alien eyes" would bring them money and fame. Or maybe Trixie was a covert "wannabe" who just wanted to play.

Lessons

WHETHER TRIXIE WAS A "PSYCHIC-POWERED MATA HARI" OR SOMETHING ELSE, the episode shows the danger of suspending disbelief and trusting the wrong person out of desire to help, or to get the "greatest UFO story of all time," or for love, for money, out of fear, or for all of the other possible reasons we can become blind to the tell-tale signs of being manipulated.

The realm of UFOs takes us straight "through the looking glass," inducing a mind-altering shift where we forget to do reality checks and listen to input from colleagues, friends, family and yes, even debunkers, who might pick up on signals we missed. ●

Abductions

AND MISSING TIME

AS BETTY AND BARNEY HILL WERE DRIVING HOME FROM VACATION IN THE AUTUMN OF 1961, Betty noticed a bright light in the night sky, as it moved erratically and grew in size. Barney grabbed his binoculars and saw a round spacecraft the size of a jetliner. Several humanoid beings were standing at the windows of the craft staring back at *him!*

Terrified, they fled. What happened next is unclear—the Hills simply *didn't remember!* All they recalled was becoming aware of a beeping sound coming from the trunk of the car and the next thing they knew, they were nearly home—and two hours had past! A radar report that tracked a UFO in the area that evening validated their sighting. The time lapse remained a mystery, even after the Hills later drove over the same route.

Nightmares

FOR THE NEXT TWO YEARS THE HILLS WERE PLAGUED BY INSOMNIA AND NIGHTMARES. Finally, in desperation they consulted with a leading Boston psychiatrist, Dr. Benjamin Simon, who employed hypnosis to help them remember what had happened during the lost two hours. The hypnosis sessions erupted into emotional catharsis as Betty and Barney separately re-experienced being aboard a spacecraft where aliens examined them with various medical-type instruments, including a needle that was painfully inserted into Betty's stomach. Telepathically the aliens told her this was to determine if she was pregnant. Amniocentisis, which is similar in method and used by physicians to determine birth defects, had not yet been developed by modern medicine.

Star Map

BETTY WAS MORE CONSCIOUS AND LESS AFRAID throughout the experience than was Barney. She spoke to one of the aliens, who showed her a map of where he was from. Under hypnosis Betty drew a duplicate of this star map, which closely matched the view of our solar system from just beyond the Zeta Reticuli star system, which she had had no knowledge of prior to the encounter.

The Betty and Barney Hill's eerie experience ushered in an era of similar accounts. It brought awareness that UFOs were not simply lights in the sky but might carry occupants intent upon interacting with humans in startling ways.

Aliens with Claws

ANOTHER CLOSE ENCOUNTER OCCURRED IN 1974. Charles Hickson and Calvin Parker were packing up after a fishing expedition along the Pasagoula River in Mississippi, when Hickson noticed a fast approaching, strange blue light. It stopped about forty yards away, hovered about ten feet off the ground, emitting a hissing sound. An oblong-shaped craft emerged out of the light and its door suddenly opened and three creatures with silvery gray skin and long arms ending in crab claws floated out. Hickson and Parker were paralyzed with fright as these beings escorted them aboard.

The light inside the craft was so bright Hickson could only make out something like a large TV screen in the wall. Unable to move or speak, he watched a crystal sphere with a metallic ball in the center of it, slowly move around him, as if it were examining his body.

When the mysterious sphere disappeared, Hickson was led outside by the beings where he found Parker in a state of shock. When they both regained their senses, they went to the nearest police station and, still extremely agitated, reported what had happened.

Telling the Truth

HICKSON AND PARKER DEMANDED THAT THEY BE EXAMINED BY LIE DETECTOR TESTS, WHICH THEY PASSED. Later, after military personnel at Keesler Air Force Base interrogated them, the police left them alone in a room with a hidden microphone in the hopes that they would reveal a conspiracy. The ploy yielded nothing. All Hickson and Parker spoke of was their fear and disbelief. Parker was later hospitalized with a nervous breakdown.

Missing Time

PIONEER ABDUCTION INVESTIGATOR, BUDD HOPKINS NOTICED A PATTERN OF "MISSING TIME" IN MANY OF THE ACCOUNTS from witnesses reporting UFO encounters. Curious, he thought hypnosis might help people retrieve memory of the time lapses. His subjects described feeling paralyzed, then floating through walls or the roof of the car, or being beamed up into a spacecraft where they encountered strange beings with large heads, huge almond-shaped eyes and gray skin. The alien creatures performed medical-like procedures on them, such as taking skin, ovum, and sperm samples, inserting needles into their heads or abdomens, and implanting small round objects in their nasal cavities or brains. Often their bodies were scanned with a device or light instrument.

Hopkins' abductee subjects reported that following the encounters they woke in their beds. Sometimes they found themselves lying in the opposite direction, or with their night-clothes on inside out. One of my clients reported having seen small, dark figures entering his bedroom before losing consciousness. He said he awoke hours later, outside his house. It was raining, yet, his pajamas were completely dry. He had no memory of what had happened or how he got there.

Screen Memories

SOMETIMES WHEN PEOPLE EXPERIENCE A UFO ENCOUNTER OR MISSING TIME, they come up with explanations that don't make sense. Sometimes it is a "screen memory"—an illusionary memory that masks what was actually seen. Under hypnosis a client I'll call Shelly remembered sitting in a parked car on a dirt road deep into the desert, when she became mesmerized by a ball of light in the distant night sky, which repeatedly come closer, then moved further away. As Shelly watched it, out of the corner of her eye she noticed a gray "parking meter" next to the driver side window.

"A parking meter? In the middle of the desert?" I questioned. Shelly's memory called for closer examination, especially since the shape and color of a typical parking meter bears an uncanny resemblance to the skull-shaped head and gray skin color of many aliens. As sometimes happens, Shelly was too frightened to explore the experience further. Typical screen memories include seeing animals with large eyes, like owls, deer, or wolves, even though the person was in a city.

Mind Scans

SOME ABDUCTEES REPORT HAVING HAD THEIR MINDS SCANNED, in which aliens stared deeply into their eyes as if they are reading their mind. Roger, for example, had reoccurring dreams in which he performed psychic readings on people by grabbing them and looking deeply into their eyes. "I look past all their presentation of who they are, and to their core. I can then tell things about them," he said. The dreams distressed Roger because he was professionally trained to do psychic readings and this invasive procedure was contrary to what he'd been taught. Later Roger was startled to read in David Jacob's book, *Secret Lives*, that aliens did "mind scans" by peering deeply and intrusively into abductees's eyes, just as he had dreamt.

Not Insane

As "far-out" as these accounts sound, most people who report having been abducted are not psychotic or otherwise mentally ill. The demographics of people reporting contact with aliens represents a cross section of socio-economic groups and professions—lawyers, farmers, nurses, police officers, politicians, even psychiatrists. Psychological tests administered to abductees have not uncovered abnormalities. Dr. John Mack, professor of psychiatry at the Cambridge Hospital, Harvard Medical School, who studied people reporting UFO close encounters found no evidence of mental illness—aside from signs of havng undergone a stressful experience. The way clients presented their experiences, reliving them in emotionally charged sessions, and the consistency between different accounts convinced him that these were real experiences. As a psychiatrist, he concluded that he was *not* seeing evidence of mental illness.

Certainly there are imaginary accounts, possibly arising from a need to explain emotional pain in one's life, or a need to feel special. I've had clients who were kind of "wannabe" abductees who had seemingly unconsciously "taken on" abduction scenarios to fulfill such emotional needs. Of course, there also are out-and-out hucksters in the UFO community, like my houseguest with the alien eyes, trying to con people into giving them power, fame, sex or money. Nonetheless, not all reports of close encounters can be explained in this way. ☺

Implants

AND TRACKING DEVICES

MANY ABDUCTEES TELL OF HAVING HORRIFYING FLASHBACKS, in which aliens used a long needle to insert some kind of small object high up into their nasal cavities. This ordeal may be accompanied by a "crunching" sound as if cartilage or bone was being penetrated. Implants may be forced under the skin on the feet or hands, behind the ears—actually anywhere.

Implants had been relegated to the murky realm of heresay and given little credibility until Dr. Roger Leir and Derrel Sims, a former CIA agent and investigator for the Houston UFO Network, joined forces in 1995 to scientifically investigate the odd phenomenon. In his book, *The Aliens and the Scalpel*, Leir tells of eight UFO experiencers who had implants surgically removed. Sims and Leir filmed and documented each surgery and described in detail the nine foreign objects removed. They varied in size and shape. Some were the size of a cantaloupe seed, or were T-shaped; others were round.

Extraterrestrial Origin

WITHOUT BEING INFORMED OF THE ORGIN OF THE IMPLANTS, New Mexico Tech was contracted to perform a series of tests on the objects, including X-ray spectroscopy and electron microscopy. Their results indicated that while one object was composed of brown bottle glass, the others were composed of calcium and other elements with iron-carbon in the cores. The lab suggested *the objects were extraterrestrial in origin,* speculating they were from meteorites because they displayed a similar composition of metals. Yet, New Mexico Tech Lab noted that the objects differed from meteorites, which could be considered natural, in that they appeared to have been engineered or artificially constructed.

How meteoric particles could have become embedded in someone's body is an unexplained mystery. It is hard to imagine that all the implant victims had been physically struck by a meteor. Not only is it statistically unlikely but such an accident would have left physical scarring and an indelible memory of the event.

Medical Analysis

ALL OF THE IMPLANTS LEIR STUDIED SHOWED SOME FLUORESCENCE. Some had been surrounded by an extremely tough, dark membrane. The medical lab analysis indicated that the membranes were made of superficial tissue composed of keratin. which is usually found only in the very outer surface of skin or in hair or finger and toenails. The lab verified that nerve ends had grown around the implants. These findings were highly unusual because nerve ends usually do not intertwine around foreign objects. Furthermore, the body doesn't develop skin-like tissue inside muscles. Another anomaly is that no sign of inflammation was evident. When a foreign object invades the body, inflammation is a side-effect of the body's natural attempt to fend off the object. Some evidence of inflammation would be expected, even when the object has been there for years.

Communion

BEST-SELLING HORROR AUTHOR WHITLEY STRIEBER FOUND TERROR INTRUDING INTO HIS LIFE IN 1985 when he experienced disturbing encounters with "visitors." It began when Strieber was awakened in the night by moving sounds. As he sat up in bed, he saw a three and a half tall figure with dark holes for eyes and a line for a mouth peering around the bedroom door. When it suddenly rushed toward him, Strieber blacked out.

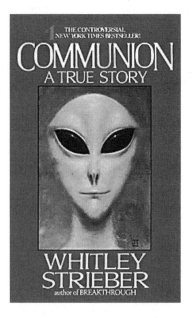

Afterwards Strieber remembered lying in a small circular chamber surrounded by small beings. One held a long needle, which it intended to insert into his head. Strieber's terror was immense. "What can we do to help you to stop screaming?" one of the beings asked. "Let me smell you," he demanded. Another being put its hand to Strieber's nose. It smelled slightly sour with a hint of cinnamon—and *not* human. The beings also inserted a triangular probe into his anus, and made an incision on his fingertip, leaving physical wounds that lingered for days.

The encounters, which included soulful communion with the visitors along with more painful medical-like procedures, continued for years. Strieber worried that he was going insane or had a brain tumor as he decended into a suicidal depression. Results from medical and psychological tests were normal, except for an MIR brain scan that revealed a small anomalous spherical object lodged in his brain. The composition of the suspected implant remains a mystery because it was too risky to be removed for analysis.

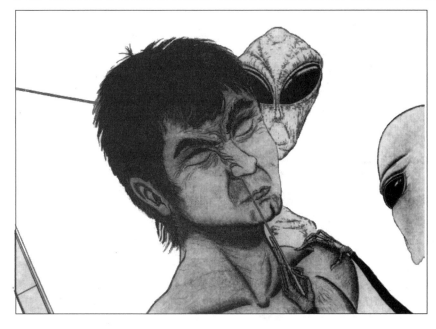

Tracking Devices?

STRIEBER REPORTED A CASE of an unknown object surgically removed from a man named Jesse Long, who had encountered a praying mantis-type being during his childhood. The object extracted from Jesse's leg looked like a sliver of glass. Detailed analysis determined that, unlike ordinary glass, the implant was composed of 99.3 percent of silica with a strange orange-peel-type surface unlike fused silica or glass. Furthermore, the implant conducted electricity which is impossible, given its composition. The lab report noted that to fuse silica at that concentration into glass requires a tremendous amount of heat. It would demand technological know-how comparable to that used to produce the insulating tiles on the outside of the space shuttle, enabling it to withstand the tremendous heat of reentry into the Earth's atmosphere.

The examining scientists speculated that the object's unique properties would enable it to transmit and receive signals similar to the way radio crystals work. The depth of the documentation of Leir's and Strieber's cases demands that, whatever the implants may be, they cannot be simply dismissed as the products of someone's imagination!

Just say, "No!"

A TRACKING DEVICE MAY HAVE BEEN IMPLANTED IN ONE OF MY CLIENTS! Jeff and I had been working on his UFO encounters regressed him to the age of nine and he relived gray aliens using a long needle to implant something into his left temple. He remembered it as being like a large grain of sand. An alien told him that it would block his memory of their encounters and keep him from "going crazy." " You'll feel calmer," the alien said, but Jeff didn't believe him.

Years later, as an adult, Jeff smashed his head against a windshield during an auto accident, which he believes crushed the implant because the aliens returned shortly after the accident and tried to convince him to let them insert another one. "It won't hurt you and you don't even use what it accesses," the aliens said, but didn't explain what its purpose really was. Jeff's impression was that the aliens now had to ask permission to replace the implant. Jeff refused. He was surprised to discover that when the aliens left he felt joyfully *alone*—for the first time since he was nine years old. He was free from their interference at last!

Maybe Beneficial

JOHN SALTER EXPERIENCED A UFO SIGHTING AND A SEVERAL-HOUR TIME LAPSE and later remembered having a short, gray alien painlessly insert an implant in his nasal cavity. Within a year of the incident, Salter noticed his facial lines receding, his skin feeling smoother and generally felt healthier, with a higher resistance to colds and minor aliments. He suddenly stopped a heavy smoking habit virtually overnight "without even thinking about it." Salter, who teaches Native American Studies at North Dakota University, firmly believes that aliens are "people" who use their expanded awareness to assist humans in the struggle to improve conditions on earth.

Love Bites

AND SEX WITH ALIENS

SOME WOMEN ABDUCTEES GIVE BIZARRE ACCOUNTS OF BEING FORCED TO HAVE SEX WITH ALIENS and subjected to artificial insemination—and becoming pregnant! A few months later they discover that they were no longer pregnant, without having had a miscarriage. Hopkins tells of a doctor's wife who had her pregnancy confirmed by reliable tests, including ultrasound. When, at the end of the first trimester, the fetal heartbeat could not be heard, surgery was performed. No fetus was found—only an umbilical cord and placenta were in evidence. The surgeon could not explain what could have happened to the fetus. The woman reported having had unusual experiences indicative of alien contact.

Lizard Lovers

JAZZ SINGER PAMELA STONEBROOKE SHOOK UP THE UFO COMMUNITY when she reported having had erotic encounters with an alien lizard. Speaking in a sultry tone, the strikingly attractive, tall, flaxen blonde projects a matter-of-fact attitude about her rather kinky amorous encounters.

**Pamela
Stonebrooke**

Stonebrooke was awakened during the night by an exceptionally handsome blond man making love to her. She said that his caresses felt so good that just she closed her eyes and relaxed. Suddenly her lover became aggressive. In shock, she watched him shapeshift into a reptilian man—staring at her with yellow, starburst pupils. She was completely under his control, yet strangely unafraid. The lizard told her telepathically that they had known each other *forever*. Hearing this, Stonebrooke completely surrendered to the experience of every cell in her body exploding into orgasm. Then her lizard lover suddenly disappeared—as if he had been pulled out of the physical dimension of the room.

Stonebrooke doesn't consider herself to be a victim or call herself an "abductee." In her book, *Experiencer: A Jazz Singer's True Account of Extraterrestrial Contact*, Stonebrooke says she believes she was a lizard being in past lives and and had agreed to continue her contact with the lizard during this lifetime. Stonebrooke's candid reports of her experiences fuels the ire of skeptics and flies in the face of the "typical" abduction scenario, accepted by ufologists. Nonetheless, when told by Stonebrooke, her galactic love affair sounds intriguing.

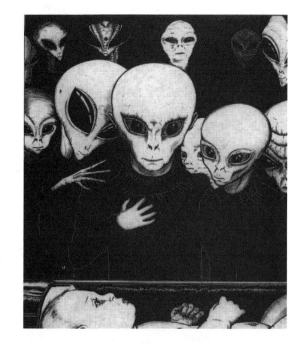

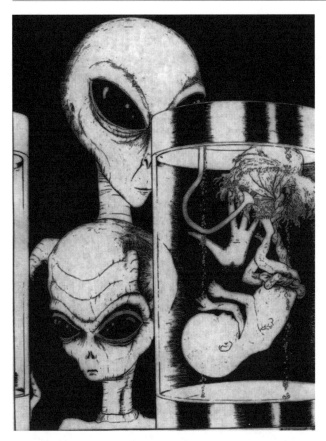

Men as Studs

Women are not alone in being alien sex objects. Some male abductees tell of having sperm samples removed with strange instruments. Others tell of mechanical sex with females with human-looking bodies and alien facial features. One of the earliest reported human-alien sexual encounters happened in the 1950s in Brazil. Villa Boaz said he found himself on board an alien craft where he had sex with a short, human-looking woman with slanted eyes, short spiky hair, and bright red public hair. Afterwards she pointed to her belly then up to the sky.

Hybrid Off-Spring

WOMEN AND MEN BOTH HAVE REPORTED BEING TAKEN aboard an alien craft, shown a hybrid child with human-alien characteristics and told it's their child. There are children who describe being taken aboard a craft and told to play with strange, hybrid-looking children while aliens watch closely how they get along with them. Pamuel Stonebrooke said she was taken aboard an alien spaceship surrounded by small gray aliens who took her to a room where four little girls grabbed her arm and called her, "Mommy." More alien-looking than human, the little girls had wispy blond hair and large dark eyes barely rimmed with white.

"Indigo Children" is a growing phenomenon. Parents of these "Star Chldren", as they are also called, report that their children seem to have unusual abilities such as being gifted or very psychic and seem to have an "otherworldly" quality and appearance. These children sometimes describe having contact with "Star People" or make references to UFOs. The implication is that alien-human hybrids may be being born into and raised in human families.

Alien Love Bite

Eve Lorgen, who has a graduate degree in counseling psychology, was working with abductees when she discovered the "love bite." She describes it as a love obsession that begins with a kind of "psychic rape" in which the person is manipulated by aliens into falling in love with another abductee. These alien arranged relationships are emotionally intense and accompanied by strong psychic connections, paranormal phenomena, and synchronicities. Although short lived, the obssessions have devastating consequences. Marriages break up, family and friends are abandoned as the obssession drives them to move across the country in pursuit of the beloved, only to have their "love" fade in a matter of weeks.

Some of Lorgen's loved-obsessed abductees describe military personnel along with aliens as their abductors. In her book, *The Love Bite: Deeper Insights in the Alien Abduction Phenomena*, Lorgen speculates that aliens, in league with military groups, may be studying genetic lines and harvesting emotional and sexual energies, which they may be utilizing to time travel, cause materializations, and enhance psychic power. Alternatively, the love bitten abductees may have been mind-controlled into becoming special operatives who, when they are "soul bonded" to another, will take greater risks, thereby improving the mission's success.

Lorgen claims that ufologists who discount the love bite phenomena are afraid to look at darker alien scenarios. I admit that I am skeptical. I have seen obsessive love affairs amongst members of the UFO community and they've looked no different from romantic dramas played out elsewhere.

Genetic Manipulation Theory

HOPKINS, JACOBS, AND OTHERS ARE CONVINCED there is a species of aliens who need genetic material from humans to fortify their survival. They hypothesize that the aliens "tag" certain people, much in the way zoologists tag animals for observation in the wild. Tagged people are periodically captured, tested, and used for genetic experimentation, with the goal of developing a hybrid alien/human race.

Hopkins concedes that the aliens probably do not have hostile intentions towards humans but insists they have a consistently negative effect and show little interest in altering their agenda. Other UFO researchers hold the view that it may be the human race that needs fortification and if a hybrid program exists, it is to help us evolve. ☺

SIGHTING CLASSIFICATIONS

Daylight Disc

Unidentified flying objects of any shape, seen during the day.

Nocturnal Light

Any unidentified light seen at night. This is the most common sighting.

Radar-Visual

An UFOs seen from the ground and tracked on a radar screen.

Close Encounter of the First Kind (CE-1)

The sighting of an unidentified object within the range of 500 feet , close enough to observe some details.

Close Encounter of the Second Kind (CE-2)

UFOs leaving physical traces, such as scorched earth, a oily substances, damaged plants, erratic animal behavior, and radiation or electromagnetic disturbances, such as car engines dying and televisions blinking off.

Close Encounter of the Third Kind (CE-3)

A sighting of alien beings but with no physical interaction with humans, usually occurring in or around UFOs.

Close Encounter of the Fourth Kind (CE-4)

Physical interaction between humans and alien beings, involving telepathic communication, medical-type procedures, information exchange, or demonstrations of certain powers or abilities.

Close Encounters

OF THE GOOD KIND

NOT ALL CLOSE ENCOUNTERS WITH ALIENS ARE NEGATIVE. Many people have profound, spiritual encounters with ETs who become positive guiding forces in their lives. Encounters with one type of beings can be beneficial while experiences with other aliens are negative. During past life regressions, some people even experience being aliens themselves!

The phrase "Close Encounters of the Fifth Kind" was coined by Steven Greer, director of the Center for the Study of Extraterrestrial Intelligence (CSETI) to refer to the successful efforts by humans to contact extraterrestrials. Greer repudiates the assumption that humans play no part in what happens during UFO sightings and refers to evidence of UFOs coming closer, leaving, or otherwise responding in perfect timing to the expressed thoughts of witnesses.

The goal of CSETI has been to develop methods for making contact with UFOs using lights, laser signals, telepathic projections, human and mechanical sounds, and other techniques. One CSETI group reported dramatic results after efforts to attract a UFO were rewarded by a craft landing about forty miles away, which left landing traces. In another incident a huge craft flew in, at close range, seemingly in response to CSETI group working in Mexico.

Greer cautions against viewing the ETs as spiritually more advanced, or conversely, assuming that humans are morally or otherwise superior. He advocates the "universe as one people" approach. He promises trying to establish communication as equals, as ambassadors of intergalactic exchange, even if we are technologically surpassed.

Greer urges that we assume that ETs' intentions are benevolent or at least neutral. Disturbing encounters described by Bud Hopkins and others notwithstanding, Greer reminds us that "actions do not equal motives." Greer, who is an emergency trauma doctor, give the example of how panicked children can experience actions of emergency medical personnel as painful and intrusive when their intention is only to help.

Healing Experiences

EDITH FIORE, A PSYCHOLOGIST WHO STUDIED THOUSANDS OF PEOPLE who have had close encounters, says that about half report being cured of illness as a result of their interaction with aliens. Psychologist turned UFO researcher, Richard Boylan estimates that 95 percent of extraterrestrial contact is positive but goes unreported because many contactees don't feel the need to seek professional assistance.

Dr. John Mack hypothesized that the abduction experience, while traumatic, may help the abductees move to a higher level of consciousness. Often abductees become concerned about saving the earth after their encounters because they remembered receiving messages from aliens about the desecration humans are perpetuating on the planet. Mack notes that while the aliens may not be trying to enlighten human beings, there is something about the phenomenon that has that effect. Mack is not alone in noticing this. Less rigorous surveys have indicated a high percentage of contactees become more actively involved with environmental issues, global peace, and spiritual pursuits. They often report becoming more psychic and intuitively aware.

Signs of Abduction

THERE ARE A NUMBER OF COMMON ELEMENTS DESCRIBED BY PEOPLE WHO REPORT CLOSE ENCOUNTERS or abductions. The experience is often set off by seeing a UFO craft , or a bright, intense light of unknown origin, especially at close range. People experience missing time, such as when driving somewhere and arriving much later than expected with no recollection of the delay.

Hopkins worked with Kathy Davies who claimed to have been abducted repeatedly. Landing traces were found in her backyard—circular marks in the ground where plants refused to grow for years. Abductees report nose bleeds and unexplained bruises. Sims found that in some cases there was a brilliant green or pink fluorescence found on the bodies of alleged abductees.

Nightmares

ABDUCTEES OFTEN HAVE REPETITIVE NIGHTMARES AND WEIRD DREAMS, particularly involving strange looking beings taking them inside a craft, or an enclosed space, or operating room where they are subjected to invasive medical procedures by "little doctors." They sometimes report hearing a high pitched buzzing in their ears. They may have memories of floating or flying through the air.

Fears and phobias are common, such as fear of the dark and going to sleep. Many abductees must have the lights on before they can go to sleep. Some become terrified just by seeing an illustration of an alien or watching a UFO movie or TV program.

Experiencing paralysis when they awaken during the night or during the sighting of a UFO-like light is a frequent symptom. People have awakened to find "scoop marks," which are small circular indentations in the skin, or red spots, cuts or rashes with a geometric pattern, or small bumps that suddenly appear without explanation.

Having any or all of these symptoms does *not* necessarily mean that you have been abducted. There can be, and usually are, other explanations. Sleep paralysis, for example, is a common, normal occurrence that generally has nothing to do with UFOs. However, if efforts to find the cause and alleviate related anxiety have been unsuccessful, there may be a possibility that you have had an encounter of the "too-close kind."

Question Reality

CLIENTS HAVE TOLD ME OF PROBES, NEEDLES, EXTRACTION OF SPERM AND OVUM, frightening scenes of being paralyzed and overpowered by beings half their size. As wierd as these experiences sound, I have been impressed by the sense of reality that emerges during some of these sessions. Night-terrors and other symptoms of post traumatic stress have abated as we explored their UFO experiences in hypnotic sessons.

It isn't clear if our physical-based reality is the *only* reality. Perhaps people can have experiences in other realms of consciousness and dimensions that can be accessed through hypnosis. The wisest approach is to explore our experiences without rushing to conclusions as to what is, or is not "real." We need to avoid the blanket assumption that all alleged abductees suffer from mental illness or are making up stories, or conversely, that there is nothing to gain from consciously or unconsciously fabricating stories of alien encounters.❍

© BREDWART '94

Alien Zoo

AND SPACECRAFT

ALIENS COME IN A WIDE VARIETY OF SHAPES AND COLORS. Most commonly reported are small, gray beings three to four feet high, with oversized heads, huge, dark, almond-shaped eyes, a slit for a mouth and virtually no nose. These are usually described as workers, even androids, who perform tasks for five-foot tall Grays or tan colored aliens with similar characteristics. One client described encountering a dragon-looking creature, which I dismissed as a confabulation until I heard other people describe encountering similar beings.

Pamela Stonebrooke tells of having out-of-this-world ecstatic sex with lizard beings, but others report malevolent and definately *non*-ecstatic encounters with lizard aliens. Reports of insectoid creatures resembling praying mantis, ants, or flies are common. There are also stories of human Nordic-looking beings with fair skin and blond hair, like Adamski's Space Brother. Some extraterrestrials are frog-like with two eyeball type antennae. Others are wrinkled and fat; yet others are robot-like biological entities. There have been reports of aliens being accompanied by humans in military uniforms—hinting that the military may have a covert allegiance with the aliens.

Shape-Shifters

THE PLETHORA OF ALIENS MAY SIMPLY REFLECT THE HUGE VARIATION OF LIFE FORMS in the universe or perhaps aliens shape-shift at will. We may be encountering a phenomenon operating in a different dimension that takes on dream-like characteristics as it mixes with projections from our own psyche. It could be the creatures are so strange that witnesses have no memory template for them, so the mind produces a hodgepodge of whatever it resembles—an insect body, a skull-type head, or a dragon—which varies from person to person, producing a vast array of descriptions.

During a hypnotic session a client was describing the outer appearance of a UFO he had sighted years earlier, when he suddenly said, "I don't understand how the ship is so much bigger on the inside than it looks on the outside." After a pause, he gasped, "How do I know that?!" Taking a deep breath, he began describing the inside of the craft even though he had no previous memory of having entered it. The "inside being bigger than the outside" has been reported by many experiencers. This client also described and drew a picture of a central column that matched descriptions by Bill Meier, Bob Lazar, and others. Those who have had contact with extraterrestrials have provided detailed descriptions of spacecraft including simplified explanations of the technology involved.

How Spaceships Travel

THE PLEIADIANS ALLEGEDLY GAVE BILLY MEIER DESCRIPTIONS OF THEIR SPACECRAFT and rudimentary explanations of how they negotiated the five hundred light years from their planet to earth—the equivalent of one thousand years travel time with our technology. They said it took seven hours—which was slow because they cannot use their hyperdrive until they are out of range of other planets.

Electro-Magnetic Energy

THE PLEIADIAN CRAFT PROPORTEDLY UTILIZES ELECTRO-MAGNETIC ENERGY TO OVERCOME INERTIA and set up its own gravitational system. They told Meier there is a protection field around the craft that neutralizes earth's gravity and allows the craft to move freely. This is why in film footage UFOs often seem to be bobbing and swaying, like a boat on water.

Inside the craft there is a central magnetic pole containing periscopic lenses for surveillance and assisting in the absorption of static power for recharging. The propulsion system relies on implosion rather than explosion, reconverting the energy it utilizes. The craft maintains its own gravity inside the ship so the occupants have no sense of movement even at tremendous speeds and angles of trajectory.

Null Time

THE PLEIADIANS SAID THAT "BEAMSHIPS," SO NAMED BECAUSE OF A LIGHT-EMITTING DEVICE which provides the power, are equipped with a normal drive which accelerates the craft up to the speed of light and a hyper-drive which propels the craft many times faster. The hyperdrive, however, causes a small tear in the fabric of time and can suck anything close to it into a time warp where it remains trapped.

When the ship reaches hyperdrive it enters hyperspace. The craft and everyone inside it are converted into high-speed particles that rematerialize into solid form when the destination is reached. In effect, time is energy and in hyperspace time and space is converted into high-speed particles which Pleiadians refer to as "null-time."

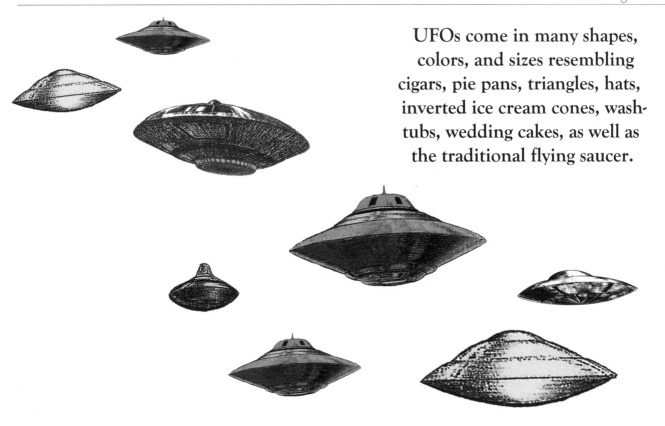

UFOs come in many shapes, colors, and sizes resembling cigars, pie pans, triangles, hats, inverted ice cream cones, wash-tubs, wedding cakes, as well as the traditional flying saucer.

Variety of Crafts

ACCORDING TO MEIER, THE BEAMSHIPS ARE JUST ONE of several types of Pleiadian crafts. There is a huge mother ship, about ten miles long which houses a community of 140,000 Pleiadians. It acts as a base to beamships, orbiting outside the planet's atmosphere. Smaller craft called "telemeter ships" are used to monitor planet activities. All ships are equipped with camouflage systems so that humans don't see them unless the Pleiadians decide to show themselves.

Element 115

BOB LAZAR'S DESCRIPTION OF THE ALIEN SPACECRAFT'S PROPULSION SYSTEM HE WORKED ON AT AREA 51 corresponds to the Pleiadian descriptions given to Billy Meier. Lazar claimed to have identified a non-radioactive substance, he called "Element 115," used in the craft's engine that has the capability to amplify gravitational waves to create a separate gravitational field around the craft that counters the earth's gravitation and allows for free, frictionless movement. Element 115 is purportedly so powerful that it can actually bend time and space in a way that allows for instantaneous travel across light years of distance.

Science is Catching Up

IN 1999, THE FRENCH COMMITTEE FOR IN-DEPTH STUDIES, COMETA, RELEASED RESULTS OF A STUDY by the French Institute of Higher Studies for National Defense on UFOs. Under the banner of "consider all of the hypotheses" it recognized that anomalous aerial phenomena could be extraterrestrial in origin. The COMETA report is firmly scientific, yet maintains an open approach to studying

UFOs. I see it as our best model for how a government can publicly investigate the field in an intelligent manner without the kind of secrecy and disinformation perpetuated by the US government.

COMETA theorizes magnetohydrodynamics (MHD) is used for propulsion. MHD utilizes an electrical current that flows around a submarine while a magnetic field is emitted, causing the water to flow in such a way that it propels the ship. Aircraft using MHD would require stronger electrical currents and magnetic fields, which would be soundless and give a luminous quality—both of which have been reported in UFO sightings. Development of MHD propulsion for aircraft is in progress in the United States, England and Russia. It is interesting the degree to which MHD corresponds to Meier's and Lazar's description of UFO propulsion systems.

Other propulsion possibilities cited by COMETA include particle beam generators, nuclear propulsions using fission, anti-matter—now a credible source—and anti-gravitational systems. These and other exiciting possibilities are being researched at the Jet Propulsion Laboratory, Lawrence Livermore Laboratory, and the Air force Astronautical Laboratory at Edwards Air Force Base. COMETA predicts that in "a few dozen years" humans will develop craft with UFO capabilities.

Experiencer's Reports

DOLORES CANNON, AUTHOR OF THE CUSTODIANS, IS A HYPNOTHERAPIST who has regressed hundreds of UFO experiencers. Her clients speak of "motherships" which do not enter the earth's atmosphere and to which humans are rarely taken. Instead, most interactions between aliens and humans take place on smaller spacecraft often staffed by small android beings who are specially engi-

Dolores Cannon

neered to withstand the slower vibrations of the earth's atmosphere that extraterrestrials have difficulty tolerating. This matches Billy Meier's report that the Pleiadians developed highly complex androids not susceptible to contaminates in the earth's atmosphere to carry out much of their work.

A client of hypnotherapist, Helen Billings, during a past life regression found herself actually *being* a UFO craft! She discovered that the craft was a living system with its own consciousness—and that's what she was. Another researcher examined a piece of metal purportedly from a UFO and realized it was not metal at all but seemed alive and plant-like. Intuitively, he began to realize that the craft was a living, biological entity that was, in effect, "grown" to fit the pilot.

Dreamtime

One night as I fell asleep I recognized that I was dreaming. In this lucid sleep-state, I decided to focus on the intention of meeting the Pleiadians. Immediately, I found myself in a round spacecraft and was startled to see it open at the top revealing a canopy of stars overhead—not at all like Meier's photos of beamships. There were human Nordic-looking beings looking at me with surprise but no words were exchanged. About a year later I attended a presentation by Randolph Winter, a spokesperson for Billy Meier, who showed a drawing of a craft that had a top that could appear invisible, giving full view of the stars. With a shock of recognition I realized that it matched the craft in my dream! Or was it a dream?

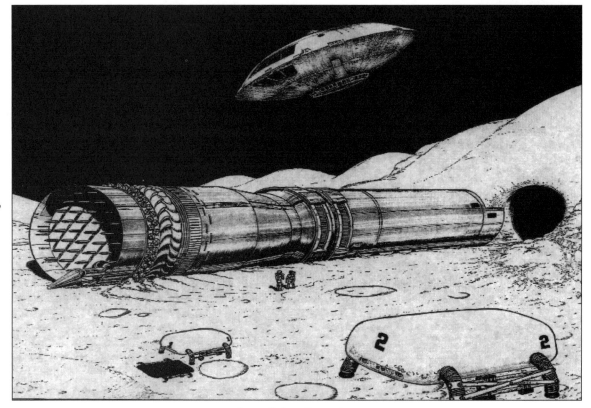

Lunar Colonies are likely to be among the first to be constructed.

Lunar Colony Expansion

IF YOU SEE A UFO

DON'T PANIC.
Take a few deep breaths and remain calm. You are probably not in danger.

BE OBSERVANT AND NOTICE DETAILS. Notice the shape, color, surface quality, size and flight pattern. Estimate the distance, speed, and elevation of the craft. Actually describing the details silently to yourself or aloud to another observer will enhance your memory.

WRITE IT DOWN. As soon as you can, write down a detailed description of what you observed. Include the time of day or night and the length of the sighting along with the location, weather conditions, cloud patterns, environment, air quality, sounds, and presence of radio towers or power lines. Make sketches and diagrams of your sighting.

PHOTOGRAPH OR VIDEO TAPE YOUR SIGHTING if you can. Include a tree, building, or other object in the picture to provide a physical reference to aid photo-analysis later.

GET ATTENTION. Call out to others. The more witnesses the better. Ask other witnesses to write down their observations *before* discussing your experiences with one another.

LOCATE OTHER WITNESSES. Ask neighbors, friends if they saw anything. Check TV and radio news reports and UFO websites that log sightings.

REPORT YOUR SIGHTING to the police and/or the Federal Aeronautics Administration (FAA) if the sighting is in the USA. Also report it to UFO organizations such as Mutual UFO Network (MUFON), Center for UFO Studies (CUFOS) and Aerial Phenomenon Research Organization (APRO). Contact information can be found online. Making official reports documents the sighting for later validation and comparison with other witness reports.

The Truth

IS OUT THERE

A MULTITUDE OF THEORIES, HYPOTHESES, AND FEVERISH BELIEFS SURROUND UFOs. Yet, paradoxically, everyone wants one tidy explanation. My feeling is that the truth lies on a continuum stretching from naturalistic explanations to metaphysical formulations. In other words, the answer is "all of the above." Each theory probably does explain some UFO sightings—but no one theory explains all of them.

The Flying-Saucers-Have-Not-Landed Hypotheses

THIS VIEW HOLD THAT THERE ARE NO ALIENS AND NO FLYING SAUCERS. UFOs are explained as natural phenomena mistakenly perceived to be UFOs, such as meteorological, astronomical, or optical events in nature. For example, cloud formations or Venus rising in a night sky distorted by fog could appear as UFOs.

Michael Persinger, a Canadian psychophysiologist, explains UFOs as *piezo-electricity*, which is an energy released when the earth moves along fault lines, compressing quartz crystals in the embedded rock. He theorizes that this energy creates balls of light in the atmosphere and may also create electrical disturbances in the human brain causing hallucinatory experiences that we imagine to be UFOs.

Advanced Technology

ANOTHER POPULAR EXPLANATION is that UFOs are military inventions of a highly classified nature. For example, the triangular shaped Stealth bomber secretly developed by the US military could undoubtedly account for certain sightings near the military bases where the Stealth was being tested. It is easy to imagine citizens getting a glimpse of futuristic craft on practice runs and thinking that they are extraterrestrial in orgin.

Human Psychology

SKEPTICS INSIST THAT HOAXERS, hustlers, cultists, hallucinations, and mass hysteria—all indelibly part of the human experience—can explain away the UFO phenomena. According to this premise, people see what they want to see or claim to see what they want others to believe. They do it for power, for fame, for money, for love, for kicks, or for reasons only Freud could decipher.

There are, however, more sophisticated psychological theories to account for UFOs. The famed Swiss psychologist Carl Jung explained UFOs as a psychic projection of the inner Self. He did not discount the possibility of UFOs being real, but focused instead on how the rise in UFO sightings after World War II could be a response to the increasing fragmentation and alienation in modern culture. Jung considered UFOs to be a collective myth or vision signaling a striving towards wholeness by humanity seeking a deeper meaning of life.

When Natural Explanations Fail

NATURALISTIC EXPLANATIONS AND PSYCHOLOGICAL THEORIES UNDOUBTEDLY ACCOUNT FOR MANY UFO REPORTS but they simply cannot explain all of the sightings. Armchair debunkers have probably been correct in asserting that a particular UFO was Venus or that a particular witness was mentally unbalanced. Such pat explanations, however, do not satisfy an airline pilot who *knows* the dancing lights he saw were *not* fireflies on the windshield, nor do they satisfy an UFO investigator who *knows* the witnesses she interviewed showed no signs of mental imbalance, nor do they convince an astronaut who *knows* that US technology is not capable of the aerial acrobatics demonstrated by an UFO he observed. So, if not all UFO reports can be explained as known phenomena—then where do we go?

Aliens-Are-Here Hypothesis

THE ALIENS-ARE-HERE HYPOTHESIS HOLDS THAT UFOS are exactly what they appear to be—visitors from other galaxies who have made Earth a stopping point on their intergalactic travels. Aliens have purportedly mastered the ability to travel through time and space in ways modern astrophysicists can only dream about. Just as we would be interested in studying humanoid beings from other planets, so, too, the extraterrestrials are curious about us. People describe seeing different kinds of aliens, so perhaps there are different races with different agendas for their vistations. Some ETs appear to be highly evolved spiritual beings who want to help humans expand their understanding and save the planet. Other beings seem to be more self-serving, or even malevolent.

Genetic Manipulation

SOME ABDUCTEES REPORT ALIENS TOLD THEM THAT ETs had genetically manipulated their own species to eliminate their emotional natures but this weakened them. To reclaim the vital essence that had been lost, they must genetically interbreed with humans. A variation on this message is that humans are becoming sterile due to pollution—it has been documented that in the past century fertility rates have dramatically dropped—and the project is to ensure the continuation of the human race.

Saving Us From Ourselves

ANOTHER THEORY MAINTAINS THAT WHEN ALIENS SAW the atom bomb explode they feared we were on the verge of causing our own extinction. In trying to prevent the Earth's destruction, they are also keeping us from tampering with forces powerful enough to harm our outer space neighbors. It is believed that they keep a low profile, using indirect forms of influence to guide us and will intercede in our affairs only if absolutely necessary to save the Earth. Some UFO enthusiasts believe that in the event of worldwide disaster aliens will rescue us by scooping up the chosen few and taking them to the safe harbor of huge motherships, then transporting these pioneers to seed a new planet.

Nordic Aliens are the most humanoid.

Regression Evidence

THE ALIENS-ARE-HERE HYPOTHESIS IS SUPPORTED BY REPORTS OF CLIENTS that I and other practitioners have worked with. During regressions some clients claim a specific star system, like Zeta Reticuli, or Pleiades, as the home of the beings with whom they have had contact. Sessions often contain themes of manipulating humans for alien agendas. Other times, guidance by spiritually advanced beings dominate the sessions. Reports based on hypnotic regression, or even waking recall, do not prove anything, of course. However, by exploring these unusual experiences, information has arisen that sometimes corresponds to similar material from an independent source or to physical evidence that can be scientifically or medically examined.

Interdimensional Realities

INSTEAD OF EXTRATERRESTRIALS FROM OTHER PLANETS TRAVELING LIGHT YEARS TO THE EARTH, the interdimensional theory postulates that UFOs are beings from other dimensions right here on Earth—existing simultaneously in the same space we also occupy. According to this view, these beings can pop in and out of our reality. Jacque Vallee explored this idea, pointing to the many parallels between descriptions of fairies, elves, angels and devils that match current descriptions of aliens. Recall the stories of "flaming chariots" and "ships with anchors" described earlier, which sound very similar to UFO sightings that we now describe in terms of our modern technology.

The interdimensional theory may account for the weird physics described in UFO sightings. For example, UFOs have been seen to shrink, or expand, suddenly appearing or disappearing, amorphous one moment and concrete the next. Such metaphysical acrobatics could be explained by the limitations of our three dimensional world encountering another dimension. Imagine, for example, if we lived in a two-dimensional world, like a flat picture on a wall. When a three dimensional ball moves through our flat picture-like world, all that we would see would be a mysterious image of a circle increasing and decreasing in size, appearing and disappearing as it moved through our flat plane. As humans inhabiting a three-dimensional world, an encounter with a fourth dimensional entity would be fraught with perceptual distortions such as objects instantaneously appearing and disappearing.

They are Us!

IN THIS VIEW UFOs ARE A KIND OF TIME MACHINE CARRYING HUMANS FROM THE FUTURE back in time. Aliens are *us* visiting from the future! If we could travel back in time to the Stone Age, imagine how scrawny and hairless we would look to them! Our technology would appear magical to these primitives. Just so, we could be viewing what the human body will evolve into and witness amazing feats of highly advanced technology.

This idea explains why aliens appear so humanoid and why they don't step in and correct our woes—if they disturbed history they might jeopardize their own existence in the future! It also accounts for their pervasive interest in us and why they are in this part of the universe.

Modern physics recognizes that time is relative. Experiments have been done with atomic clocks, leaving one on the ground, taking the other in an aircraft for several hours. The clock in the airplane moves more slowly than the one on the ground. If time is a relative commodity, humans may yet discover how to manipulate it to their advantage.

Hypnosis

AS A DOORWAY

BACK IN THE 1890S DURING A FLAP OF LIGHTS AND CIGAR SHAPED CRAFT FLYING OVER the United States, a Missouri man claimed he was held hostage by strange beings who used hypnosis to keep him aboard the craft. This early abduction account matches contemporary reports of aliens staring into abductee's eyes hypnotically as they perform medical-like procedures or induce amnesia. It is believed that hypnotic regression that practitioners, like myself, utilize helps unlock memories of such close encounters. The theory is that hypnosis induces the same state of mind as the original experience when the suggestion to forget was implanted.

Hypnosis is a natural altered state ranging from being fully awake to being asleep. When we go to sleep at night and awaken in the morning, we move through trance states—as we do when daydreaming, watching TV, and driving while lost in thought. In this relaxed state, the conscious mind drifts, allowing unconscious memories, images, and associations to come into awareness.

Caution

HYPNOSIS IS NOT PARTICULARLY DANGEROUS—AS SOME WOULD HAVE US BELIEVE—EVEN SO, hypnotic regressions should be performed by someone who has professional hypnosis training and experience working with psychological processes. UFO experiences can be traumatic and the practitioner must be skilled in dealing with profound emotions. The hypnotist's beliefs and values can influence the experience. As a hypnotherapist, my role is to help my clients discover the details and nature of their experiences. They must decide for themselves if it is real, beneficial or harmful, and how to best integrate it into their lives. I facilitate the process and actively work to avoid imposing my expectations onto their experience.

Can people make things up under hypnosis? Yes! Could an UFO abduction experience be a false memory? Yes! One of the first things I do with a new client is to explain that just because something emerges under hypnosis does *not* mean it is a "real" or a "true" physically-based event. Hypnosis is not a truth serum. The unconscious mind can bring up symbolic imagery in response to needs and expectations, without caring about "the truth." Hypnosis is simply a tool that brings forth material to be examined further for potential personal meaning and whatever might correspond to facts in a case or corroborate other accounts.

Hypnosis is, however, a proven tool to improve memory recall. It has been used to assist in finding lost objects, recall details of childhood experiences, and improve memory for examinations. It is increasingly common for criminal investigators to use hypnosis to assist witnesses and victims in remembering details of crimes, such as license plate numbers or an assailant's appearance. These recovered memories can give police leads to catch criminals, but are not accepted as evidence in court.

My X-Files

By strange co-incidence, my first client with UFO experiences described encounters with praying mantis beings—much like the one that appeared in my dream years earlier and started me on this path. Rick came to me because he was bothered by childhood memories of "little doctors" who came out of a closet to operate on him. He had been molested as a child and had dealt with this in psychotherapy. Nonetheless, memory of the little doctors continued to haunt him. During hypnotic regressions Rick relived a series of encounters with aliens.

Under hypnosis, Rick described a frightening encounter with a large, muscular being with an insect-like head, wearing gray boots. The being calmed Rick down by holding his shoulder then—just when Rick relaxed—suddenly thrust his hand fiercely against Rick's chest until it felt like his heart stopped. The alien inserted a spur with yellowish tentacles into Rick's genitals and extracted his sexual energy, leaving him feeling violated and robbed of an intensely personal, vital essence. After this excruciating experience the being disappeared and the pain subsided.

While still in trance, I suggested that he tune into the meaning of this event. Benevolent praying mantis-looking beings appeared in his mind, who said, "We will restore that which had been taken. Because of your early molestation experiences you have been vulnerable to unscrupulous beings who could rob you of a vital essence." They gave him advice on how to protect himself. After the session Rick said that he felt restored—and greatly relieved.

George's Experience

DURING HYPNOTIC REGRESSION, ANOTHER CLIENT GEORGE RELIVED CAMPING OUT WITH A GROUP OF PEOPLE when a craft hovered over them. Something "sucked them up" into the UFO, where he saw a rounded interior filled with benches and a lot of activity going on. He described beings with pointed chins and triangular heads with large, thin bodies of a bluish gray color wearing tight gray clothing.

George described sitting in front of a box, like a video game, and being "reprogrammed." The process seemed designed to remove emotional judgements, especially about aliens, so that he could deal with the experience without going insane. Yet, the process didn't feel right—like part of his identity had been erased.

George's experience echos reports by other abductees who had aliens tell them they had eliminated emotions. They said that while it created greater equanimity and made for a peaceful society, something vital was lost.

Alien in the Past

IT IS IRONIC THAT MANY PEOPLE WHO DEEPLY BELIEVE IN REINCARNATION can't accept the existence of UFOs, while many UFO enthusiasts discount past lives as pure imagination. Aliens and UFOs have a way of showing up in past life regressions even when neither the client nor the hypnotherapist is expecting it. Hypnotic trance seems to transcend the usual time-space perceptions so that anything seems possible. While such accounts do not "prove" anything, they do follow a centuries old practice of using trance to explore other possible realms of existence.

One hypnotherapist reported that during a past life regression she asked the client to look down and describe his footwear—a standard technique to ascertain the time period. After a long pause the client whispered, "I don't have any feet —just kind of claws" and went on to describe himself as an alien being with a humanoid body with claw-like hands and feet.

During a hypnotic regression, Ann described a lifetime when she was an alien living on another planet outside our solar system and how it felt home to her in a way Earth never had. Ann wept as she described a complete integration into a family of aliens, as if they all shared a group mind, which was utterly different from the painful isolation she was experiencing this time around, as a human.

Robert relived a past life in the desert near Jericho, long before the birth of Christ. Like his grandfather and father before him, he was the caretaker of a "technological temple," which he guarded at the bidding of strange beings he believed were angels. Contention developed among the beings and one night the sky suddenly filled with lights and fierce activity, as if a battle were underway. One group of beings ordered him to keep the temple open, others ordered him to shut it down. Racked by indecision, Robert choose tradition and kept the temple open. The temple erupted in a horrendous explosion—killing Robert. While still in trance, he reviewed this life and realized that the meaning for him was to not let tradition make his decisions for him. ◐

Signs of a Close Encounter

THERE ARE A CLUSTER OF SIGNS AND SYMPTOMS commonly described by people who have reported close encounters. A Roper survey revealed that two percent of the US public claimed having some of these experiences, indicating that as many as fifty American adults *may* have been abducted! Taken singularly the signs are not so unusual, but a preponderance of signs with no other explanation could indicate you *may* have had close contact with an extraterrestrial. Remember, however, even having all of these experiences does not necessarily mean you have been abducted.

Sighting Unidentified Objects and Lights

SEEING A BRIGHT, INTENSE LIGHT in the sky of unknown origin. Witnessing balls of light floating through your house or elsewhere. Sighting an UFO craft.

Experiencing Missing Time

MISSING TIME OF AN HOUR OR MORE. Suddenly realizing you are driving in a different direction or area with an inexplicable time lapse. Waking up in a location other than where you went to sleep or facing the opposite end of the bed.

Unexplained Physical Signs

FINDING SCARS, "SCOOP MARKS," CUTS, BUMPS, BRUISES, GEOMETRIC RASHES OR RED SPOTS on your body and having no explanation for what caused them. Frequent nose bleeds, genital soreness especially when awakening, spontaneous termination of a pregnancy with no signs of miscarriage. Hearing tones, buzzing, pulsation, or ringing in the ears.

Weird Dreams and Disturbed Sleep

HAVING DREAMS OF ALIENS, UFOS, OPERATING ROOMS, MEDICAL PROCEDURES, "little doctors," animals with big eyes like owls, wolves, or other creatures. Having dreams or memories of flying or floating through the air or moving through walls or closed windows. Experiencing paralysis on the verge of sleep or awakening while perceiving or sensing someone in the room. Feeling drugged when awakening in the morning.

Inexplicable Anxiety and Fears

FEELING AFRAID TO SLEEP, ANXIOUS IN THE DARK, fearful of large eyed creatures or pictures of aliens, panicked about medical procedures. Having a strong aversion to the subject of UFOs or aliens, or conversely, feeling obsessed with and compelled to read about UFOs or aliens.

Flashbacks and Odd Experiences

HAVING REPETITIVE FLASHBACK-TYPE IMAGES OF ALIEN FACES OR EYES, medical instruments, or examination tables. Suddenly being telepathic, having precognition, or psychokinetic abilities like affecting electromagnetic devices or lights. Hearing voices or seeing visions.

Having an Unusual Sense of Mission

FEELING "SPECIAL" OR "CHOSEN" or that you have a special mission to perform. Having a strong cosmic or global awareness. Being drawn to Buddhism, ecology, or other forms of social and spiritual consciousness. ☿

What Happens

DURING REGRESSION?

DURING A REGRESSION THE CLIENT IS GUIDED BACK IN TIME TO RE-EXPERIENCE AN EARLIER EVENT—whether it happened yesterday, twenty years ago, or another lifetime. For particularly good hyponotic subjects the original sights, sounds, physical sensations, thoughts and emotions are evoked. Forgotten memories may emerge, to release a flood of buried feelings, providing the person with a deeper understanding of what happened.

Screening

NOT EVERYONE IS A GOOD CANDIDATE FOR HYPNOSIS. One time, for example, a fellow named Ian requested hypnosis after he thought he'd been abducteed. During the assessment interview he said that he was an avid Star Trek fan, claimed the actors were talking directly to him, and he was seeing a psychiatrist. Ian was *not* a good candidate for hypnosis. Taking medication, or even being psychotic, does not mean that a person is not also being visited by aliens, but people must be able to manage physically-based, consensus reality before exploring material that could exacerbate their delusions.

Suppose "Mary" calls me, saying she worries she's been abducted. I ask Mary about what happened. Suppose Mary explains that she saw an UFO, has had weird dreams and found a sccop mark on her skin. I ask certain questions, including what she hopes to gain from hypnosis, to ascertain if she is a good candidate for regression.

Preparation

MARY MUST BE PREPARED FOR HYPTNOTIC REGRESSION, SUCH AS HAVING APPROPRIATE EXPECTATIONS. Many people worry that hypnosis will take them over and they will lose control. This is not the case. Mary will not lose consciousness when in a hypnotic trance. Part of her conscious mind will remain aware and can question, comment on, and even criticize the process. "Hypnotic regression," I explain to Mary, "can be likened to watching a movie with a friend who talks to you during the movie, asking questions like, 'Who directed this picture?' 'Is it based on a real story?' 'Who is that actor?' So you tell your friend, "Let's talk about it after the movie and just watch for now." In a similar fashion, the conscious mind may butt in to question and judge the hypnotic experience, but with practice you learn to set intruding thoughts aside and simply observe the images arising from your unconscious mind.

What is "Truth"?

MEMORY IS TRICKY. A memory can be quite clear, only later you find out it wasn't that way at all. Other times a memory can seem more imagined than real—when it really did happen. We discuss this and I caution Mary to not summarily accept everything that emerges during trance as "the truth," but to allow time to think it through. At the same time she should not censor her experience but to simply describe what comes up without trying to "figure it out" during the actual hypnotic experience. Instead, we will analyze the images together, after the regression, to determine its significance.

Trace Formation

LIKE EVERYTHING, BECOMING HYPNOTIZED IS A LEARNING PROCESS. Some people flow with it easily, others must learn how to "go into trance," such as by setting intruding thoughts aside. How a person accesses inner information is an individual matter. Visually oriented people experience vivid images whereas some people are auditory or more tactile and may not visualize but only experience sounds, impressions, or feelings.

Keep a Journal

I INSTRUCT MARY TO WRITE DOWN WHAT SHE REMEMBERS ABOUT HER UFO EXPERIENCES and any unusual events that have happened throughout her life—even if they do not seem related. This gives a record of everything Mary remembered prior to doing hypnosis and can be used as a kind of baseline. We review Mary's journal together, filling in missing details.

Inner Safe Place

HYPNOTIC TRAINING BEGINS WITH GUIDING MARY IN DEVELOPING A COMFORTABLE, SAFE INNER PLACE. Examples include an image of the ocean, or thinking about being in a wooded meadow, or imagining swaying in a hammock. Once established in Mary's mind, she can go to her inner safe place, at will, whenever she wants to feel relaxed.

Communication Signals

TALKING DURING THE TRANCE EXPERIENCE ENGAGES THE CONSCIOUS MIND, which can interfere with informtion retrieval. While hyptonized, I will guide Mary's subconscious mind in developing finger movements to indicate "yes" and "no" responses to my quesitons. These signals allow an unintrusive way to check with Mary's usubconscious mind to confirm that she is ready to explore a particular UFO encounters. When the response is "no," it is important to uncover what is needed or getting in the way. Memory of a distrubing childhood experience may have surfaced and need to be addressed or an anxiety must be allayed, for example.

Contactees sometimes feel reluctant to talk about their UFO encounters because they feel sworn to secrecy by the aliens. Should Mary have this concern, I would remind her that she has the right to know what has happened to her. Our memories are ours and we all have a right to explore them. There are hypnotic techniques that can be used to move Mary beyond such fears or blocks, but hypnosis, responsibly used, is never forced. Mary must be ready before we delve deeply into using regression.

Going Back in Time

MARY'S HYPNOTIC REGRESSION BEGINS WITH HER LYING DOWN ON A COMFORTABLE COUCH. The lights are dimmed. I speak to Mary in a soothing tone, suggesting that she notice her breath and allow her muscles to relax. Gradually Mary will become less aware of the room, her attention will drift as she listens to my voice. She may lose track of what I am saying, as various images and thoughts flow through her mind. Mary knows she is in my office, but it ceases to become important as the images and sensations coming into her awareness become more engaging. The trance state is utterly familiar, like being on the verge of sleep.

I guide Mary back to the UFO incident and ask her to describe, step-by-step, what she see, hears, and feels as if it were happening in present time. Even though some part of Mary knows that the experience it is not currently happening but there is an immediacy to it. Should the recall of the experience threaten to become overwhelming I will remind her, "Just keep describing what happened. You did get through it. You are safe now." I ask Mary's subconscious to signal with her finger when it is time to bring the regression to a close and guide her back to her safe, inner place.

De-briefing

WHEN MARY HAS FINISHED DESCRIBING HER EXPERIENCES, we explore issues that arose to determine what is helpful for her to understand about it. It is at this point—after the trance—that we delve into issues like if the memory was "real" and what it means. It is vital that Mary not feel alone in her paradigm shattering experiences. We will continue to have sessions until Mary feels she has gleaned all pertinent information and is ready to continue to integrate her esperiences on her own. ☾

Grisly

ANIMAL MUTILATIONS

A MACABRE COMPONENT TO UFO PHENOMENA IS THE GRUESOME SPECTACLE of mutilated animals. The cause of these animals' demise is unknown but the evidence is real and leaves in its wake corpses that can be subjected to whatever analysis humans have the courage and ability to perform. Cases of animals found mutilated were recorded in the 1800s, with occasional references in preceding centuries. The first animal mutilation that received wide publicity was in 1967 when a horse named "Lady" was found dead with the skin stripped off her neck. The doctor who examined Lady and analyzed tissue samples said the chest organs had been removed in a precise, surgical way.

There was no blood in the animal or on the ground surrounding the corpse. Stranger yet was the tissue analysis, which revealed that the cuts on the horse's flesh had a hard, darkened edge—as if made by high heat. This was years before lasers were used for surgery. Even with today's technology, a machine powerful enough to run a surgical laser would be about the size of a large desk, hardly something easily taken into a horse pasture.

BLT Research Team

*Mutilated bull investigated by the BLT Research Team.
The bull's muzzle is excised and its eye was removed.*

Always No Blood

ANIMAL MUTILATIONS CONTINUE TODAY ALL OVER THE
WORLD. Usually the flesh is removed in the area around
the jaw, leaving the remainder of the head intact. Cuts
often have a serrated edge or are smooth with a hard-
ened edge, suggesting they were caused by high heat
similar to what was found on poor Lady. Local au-
thorities who examined cattle corpses—some still warm
to the touch—describe "cookie cutter cuts" where ears,
eyes, sexual organs, and rectum have been cored out.
Generally the tongue has been removed from deep
within the throat. There is a consistent lack of blood
or body fluids in the animal or anywhere near it.
Investigations have found no traces of footprints, tire
tracks and no evidence to suggest that the animals
have been dragged to their final location.

Linda Moulton Howe, an award-winning filmmaker
studied the phenomenon for over fifteen years, collecting interviews, police and veterinarian
reports, as well as photographs. She investigated numerous cases in Alabama, which corre-
sponded with UFO sightings there in the early 1990s. In her documentary, *A Strange Harvest*,
Howe showed a pregnant cow that, in addition to the usual removal of organs, was cut in
such a way that the embryonic sac was fully visible. The calf fetus was still inside but there
was no fluid inside the sac or on the ground, and no blood was seen in either of the animals.

Efforts to Protect Fail

DISTRAUGHT CATTLE RANCHERS HAVE FORMED VIGILANTE GROUPS TO PROTECT THEIR ANIMALS. In one incident armed men stood watch over livestock during the entire night. Nonetheless, cattle were found mutilated the next morning. In another incident, a rancher who kept his prize bull in a corral thirty feet from his house woke up one morning to find the animal mutilated in a field of freshly fallen snow with no trace of tracks.

The theory that natural animal predators are to blame has to be dismissed, because it does not explain the surgical incisions and bloodless nature of the bodies nor does it address the lack of tracks. Another popular theory is that the animals were mutilated during satanic rituals. But this also fails to account for the evidence found at mutilation sites.

There have been a number of incidents in which tissue and organs have been mysteriously removed after the dead animal was found. In one case, a mutilated animal was found with its tongue and jaw removed. Upon returning to the site a day later, field researchers found that the cow's teats had been excised. A few days later the muscles on one side of the head and shoulders were neatly and cleanly sliced off. None of these wounds resembled those made by natural predators.

Are UFOs Involved?

UFO SIGHTINGS AND ABDUCTION CASES HAVE BEEN REPORTED IN CONJUNCTION WITH ANIMAL MUTILATIONS. The original case of Lady, for example, was in San Luis Valley of Colorado where there have been ongoing reports of darting lights in the night skies. A spacecraft the size of a football field emitting an eerie, orange light was seen hovering over a ranch in the area. Light beams were observed going down into fields and strange humanoid beings glimpsed moving about. Dark helicopters were seen buzzing over the fields during the day and night. Some witnesses tell of having been frightened by bigfoot-like creatures, eight or nine feet high, lumbering in the woods.

Scientific Analysis

SAMPLES OF SOIL AND PLANTS TAKEN from the sites where mutilated cattle were found have been analyzed by the BLT Research Team which specializes in investigating anomalous phenomena. Their analysis revealed that the plant cells appear to have been subjected to high heat which can account for alterations in their structure that do not occur naturally. Interestingly, the BLT Research Team found the same pattern of changes in samples of plant cells taken from inside crop circles.

In soil samples collected at mutilation sites, the BLT Research Team found that microscopic magnetic particles were densely congregated around the animal, becoming less dense with distance from the mutilation site. Nancy Talbott, organizer of the BLT team, explained that the particles are spherical which indicates that they have dropped through the atmosphere in a molten state—indicating the presence of an unknown heat agency located in the sky. Increased amounts of these magenetic particles are also found at crop circles and UFO "nests," or alleged landing sites.

Talbott described a landmark case, which occurred in Red Bluff in northern California in 1997. A mutilated cow was found in a steep, rocky ravine with no roads and nowhere for helicopters to land. After a couple of days the animal appeared to have been re-mutilated. Upon closer inspection field researchers found small, dark particles adhering to the hide of the cow.

When these were analyzed by infrared spectroscopy they were found to be pure bovine hemoglobin. This is significant because hemoglobin is a part of whole blood that can only be extracted through laboratory procedures. This finding eliminated natural predators as an explanation. It also is highly improbable that humans could have carried out such a technical procedure in the out-of-doors, or that someone would have carried hemoglobin to such an obscure location to sprinkle on the carcass.

The presence of pure bovine hemoglobin has disturbing implications. For one thing, it is the medium used for invitro fertilization, which is a process that involves culturing human embryos. There are similarities between cattle and humans that make them useful in genetic studies. The BLT Research Team's findings provides eerie support for the theory that extraterrestrials use the blood, organs, and tissues of cattle for "growing" alien-human hybrids and conducting genetic experimentation. Another hypothesis is that aliens are using animal fluids and tissue to gauge levels of toxins in their efforts to monitor the effects of pollution on earth.

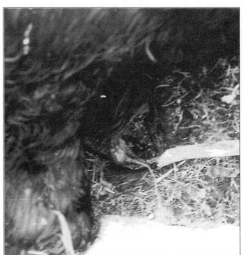

Stick points to excision area where the bull's testicles had been removed.

Animal mutilations seem to come in waves, with or without accompanying UFO sightings. There are indications that there are more sightings than are reported because people are afraid to admit to all that they have seen. ☺

Frightening

CHUPACABRAS

THE DARK SIDE BECAME EVEN DARKER WHEN REPORTS STARTED COMING IN FROM PUERTO RICO, Mexico, and southwestern areas of the United States of blood-sucking creatures destroying domestic animals and terrifying their owners. They were dubbed *chupacabra*, which is Spanish for "goat-sucker." A "vampire bird" was seen in Puerto Rico on numerous occasions in 1989. Six years later, Jaime Torres described seeing a bizarre creature in a tree glaring at him through large, dark, slanted eyes. It had a large, rounded head, devoid of hair or fur, with clawed hands and a tail, and made a hissing sound, which made him feel faint before the thing ran off into jungle brush. A few days later, in another area, a gray three-foot tall creature was seen by a number of people who said that something about the creature made them all feel sick. One child lost consciousness.

B-Grade Horror

CHUPACABRA STORIES REMINDED ME OF B-GRADE HORROR MOVIES and at first I dismissed them as the product of overactive imaginations. No one has trapped, killed, or photographed any of these creatures, after all. But what about the numerous dead animals found without a trace of blood in their bodies? The first public report was of eight dead sheep, devoid of blood, with puncture marks in their chests. Since

*EVIDENCIA OVNI
Puerto Rico*

the first recorded occurrence in 1995, deceased animals have filled newspaper reports: twenty-eight rams in Mexico, forty animals near Miami, cows in Sinalos, goats in Texas, dogs, cats and chickens—all found bloodless with puncture marks.

Ruben Uriate, Northern California Director of MUFON, went to Puerto Rico to meet with a veterinarian who showed him the results of a necropsy of a large bird that revealed long tunneling puncture marks beginning in the bird's neck and going deeply into the body cavity where certain organs were missing. It appeared as though the straw-like tongue, described by witnesses of the chupacrabra, penetrates into the body of the victim animal and consumes major organs. The vet examined a dead bull with its liver removed and found a four-inch hole in its back. He said there were claw marks on its back and footprints of a three-toed creature were seen on the surrounding ground. The creature would have to have considerable strength to overtake a bull!

The police in Sinaloa, Mexico reported shooting at a creature with a human-like face and red eyes. A police officer in San Benito, Texas saw a huge white bird, with a wingspan of close to fifteen feet, flying over the street lights. Large, dark, bat-like birds have been seen in Texas. Three-toed tracks, six inches wide and twelve inches long, were left by one of these birds in Harlington, Texas and were filmed by Ray Norton, the news director for television station KGBT. The trail went for eight feet before suddenly disappearing. There has been no direct link, however, between these sightings and dead animals, nor do the descriptions match those of the chupacabras seen in other countries.

El chupasangre or blood sucker, described by witnesses in Estanzuela, Zacupa, Guatemala, C.A.

reprinted from Evidencia OVNI
Puerto Rico

Hispanic Connection

CURIOUSLY, REPORTS OF CHUPACABRA SEEM TO CENTER MAINLY AROUND HISPANIC POPULATIONS. In addition to reports from Puerto Rico and South America, cases in the United States have come from Spanish speaking communities in New York and Boston, as well as the Southwest. So far, no one has put forth a clear theory to explain this connection. One possibility is that some Hispanic communities may have more domesticated animals, which might lure such creatures. Perhaps there is a cultural factor that sets up a predisposition for Hispanic people to encounter such creatures, which Anglo culture does not share. Another possibility is that Hispanic people are more willing to talk about what they have seen.

Genetic Experiment

SOME SPECULATE THAT THE CHUPACABRA was originally the result of genetic experimentation by the United States—or perhaps other countries—who have established research facilities in such places as Puerto Rico in their efforts to keep a low profile. The chupacabras may be the "escapees" of such experiments. It is uncertain, however, whether genetic engineering has reached a state of development as advanced as this phenomenon would indicate. The Department of Agriculture in Mexico made the official statement that the animals' deaths were caused by dogs or coyotes but—as with animal mutilations—this explanation is pathetically inadequate in explaining the condition of the bodies and other facts surrounding the cases.

reprinted from
Evidencia OVNI
Puerto Rico

George Jones' conception of a chupracabra.

Not Mutilation

CHUPACABRA ATTACKS ARE DIFFERENT FROM ANIMAL MUTILATIONS. In both cases the animals are found depleted of blood, but victims of chupacabra do not have the flesh stripped off or the organs cored out as occurs in mutilations. Victims of chupracabra show signs of a predator attack, including claw marks on the body and nearby footprints. Eye witnesses reports of seeing bizarre creatures and tracks on the ground verify the presence of *something*. By contrast, in animal mutilations the damage to the animal is made with clean cuts and surgical preciseness. There are no claw marks on the animal. Tracks have never been found and no one has ever come forth as a witness to one the these grisly events.

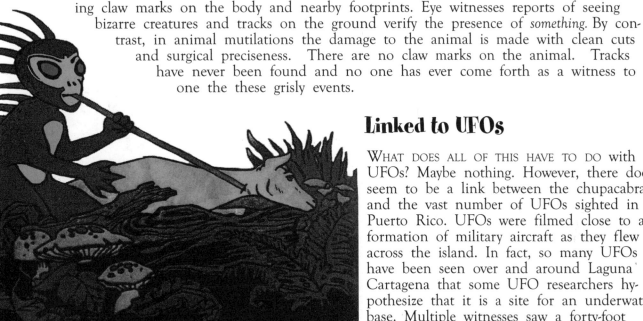

reprinted from Evidencia OVNI, Puerto Rico

Linked to UFOs

WHAT DOES ALL OF THIS HAVE TO DO with UFOs? Maybe nothing. However, there does seem to be a link between the chupacabras and the vast number of UFOs sighted in Puerto Rico. UFOs were filmed close to a formation of military aircraft as they flew across the island. In fact, so many UFOs have been seen over and around Laguna Cartagena that some UFO researchers hypothesize that it is a site for an underwater base. Multiple witnesses saw a forty-foot glowing disc in 1995 by the transmitter tower of Radio Procer in Barranquites. The radio station's equipment reacted erratically causing electronic devices to spin out of control. Witness reported seeing small, unidentifiable animals during the event. Although they did not match the usual description of chupacabra, the link between UFOs and bizarre creatures continues.

Strange Looking

DESCRIPTIONS OF THE CHUPACABRA VARY FROM UPRIGHT DINOSAURS without tails to kangaroo-like creatures with tails. The eyes are red or black, and can glow in the dark. It has spikes, or quills along the top of the head, down the back, with the arms and legs ending in three claws. Sometimes protruding fangs are visible and a long, straw-like tongue that seems designed for sucking.

UFO investigator Jorge Martin's rendition based on the description of Madelyne Tolentino who saw a Chupacabra in 1995.

© 1995 Jorge Martin

Awesome

CROP CIRCLES

ENGLAND HAS BEEN HOME TO A MYSTERIOUS PHENOMENA KNOWN AS "CROP CIRCLES," which are strange formations appearing in fields of oats, wheat, barley and canola. What began as simple circular shapes are now called "agriglyphs" because of their hieroglyphic appearance. The size, complexity and quantity of the crop circles defy charges that they are solely the products of hoaxers. By the early 1990s, over three thousand crop formations had been documented in England with hundreds reported each year since. Crop circles have also been spotted throughout the world, from rice paddies in Japan to sapling trees in Canada.

No Stalk Broken

INSIDE FORMATIONS THE OFTEN BRITTLE, SPINDLY STALKS OF GRAIN are bent or folded but unbroken and the delicate blossoms, when present, are undisturbed. The plants continue to grow, often horizontally, depending on the age of the plant. The grain is often interwoven in a complex manner with multiple vortices swirling in opposite directions, or a "basket weave" pattern emerges. Even hoaxers claiming responsibility for some of the crop circles—and undoubtedly did make some—have been unable to replicate these effects.

Ruben Uriarte

Under the Microscope

EXTENSIVE ANALYSIS BY THE BLT RESEARCH TEAM INDICATES THE LIKELIHOOD OF MULTIPLE ENERGY SYSTEMS being involved in creating crop circles. Microwaves, electrical pulses, and magnetic energy may be at work. When Dr. William Levengood, a biophysicist on the BLT Team, subjected grain stalks to microwaves, steam was created in the cells that caused the nodes to stretch, bending the stalks with no breakage, replicating the same effect found seen in crop circle grain.

BLT Research Team

The grain is often interwoven in a complex manner with multiple vortices swirling in different directions, with layers underneath swirling in the opposite direction.

The BLT Research Team discovered that crop circle plants deprived of light and water for up to eight days continue to thrive, while plants selected from outside of crop circles have died. Seeds from mature plants found in crop circles grow up to five times the normal rate, while seeds in immature plants have a markedly reduced growth rate.

Microscopic magnetic particles found in soil samples taken from inside of crop circles match those in soil samples taken from animal mutilation sites and from UFO landing traces. Interestingly, these particles originate from meteors. The spherical shape of the magnetic particles found in crop circles indicates that they were exposed to an intense heat source in the atmosphere, became molten then cooled as they fell to earth, forming spheres in the process.

Plasma Theory

A PLASMA IS A NATURALLY OCCURRING, high temperature ionized gas that contains magnetic fields, electrical pulses and microwaves, all of which have been linked to crop circles. Levengood suggests that once these plasmas are formed they rotate around the earth's magnetic field lines, being drawn to the earth's surface in various locations, perhaps due to localized geo-magnetic or ground electrical variations or abnormalities. He theorizes that this could account for some of the complex patterns seen in the crop circles. Likewise the microscopic magnetic particles are meteoric dust, which are filtering down to earth all the time, that are drawn into the plasma system by magnetic fields.

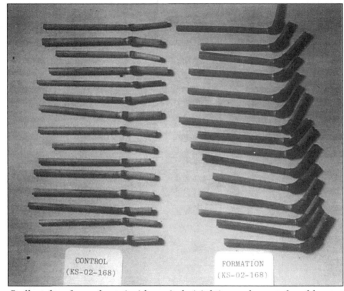

Stalks taken from plants inside a circle (right) are elongated and bent at the nodes, which is not seen in stalks taken from plants outside the circle (controls).

Is this theory the answer to the crop circle mystery? The jury is still out. Meanwhile, the strange lights and spacecraft sometimes seen hovering over crop circles have led to speculations about a UFO connection. UFOs have been sighted before and after the appearance of crop circles. Talbott, from the BLT Research Team, investigated crop circles that appeared in a small Canadian town. Every person but one that she interviewed spontaneously reported witnessing UFO activity—yet had been afraid to tell anyone else about it! Talbot strongly suggested they talk with one another about their UFO experi-

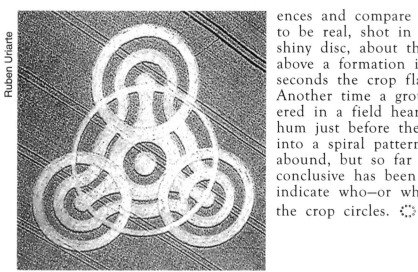

Ruben Uriarte

ences and compare notes. I watched a video, claimed to be real, shot in broad daylight, showing a small shiny disc, about the size of a tennis ball, flying above a formation in a field of grain. Within seconds the crop flattened into a formation. Another time a group of ufologists gathered in a field heard a high pitched hum just before the grass laid itself into a spiral pattern. Stories abound, but so far nothing conclusive has been found to indicate who—or what—makes the crop circles.

GLASSER

GLASSER

Many Questions
FEW ANSWERS

EXPLORATION OF UFO PHENOMENON TAKES TOLERATING A HIGH DEGREE OF UNCERTAINTY. UFO experiences are not confined to hard-edged reality or to purely psychological explanations. Skeptics resolve this uncertainty by denying their existence altogether. True believers cope with the ambiguity by adopting a spiritual cosmology incorporating all the "answers." Both sides seem to be blind to evidence that challenges their respective belief systems. Yet, the UFO phenomenon never fails to defy all assumptions.

In his book *Angels and Aliens*, Keith Thompson postulates that UFOs are a modern myth in the making. They are shapeshifters, who delight in answering only the exact question put to them, thus bewildering us with a myriad of conflicting answers. Each answer appears true, but may sharply conflict with the answer to an earlier question. Thus, Donald Menzel dismissively finds an answer of fireballs and fireflies; Billy Meier calmly takes full color photos of beamships; and Stan Friedman shakes his fist at top secret documents revealing a government cover-up. It is essential to ask questions, but we must question our questions. "Why we are asking these particular questions and not others?"

A 360-degree comprehension means continually shifting our perspective. Each witness, researcher, and enthusiast holds a different piece of the puzzle. Putting the pieces together requires cooperatively pooling information, with a sense of community, rather than fighting bitterly over who is right and wrong and what is real and what isn't.

If a cosmic intelligence wanted to push us beyond our dichotomous "either/or thinking", what better approach than employing the ambiguities of UFO phenomena? If UFOs were merely mysterious lights or objects flying overhead perhaps we could limit our search to simply proving their existance. Meteors, for example, were reported for centuries but science flatly rejected the notion of rocks falling out of the sky—until, at last, their existence was validated. But UFOs are complex, elusive and indicate intelligence in their construction and movement. They are accompanied by reports of strange beings and bizarre pheomena like animal mutilation, chupacabras and crop circles. They defy the known laws of the universe and make us question our place in it

The Western scientific paradigm says if you can't dissect it, classify and catalog it then it doesn't exist. If we remain tethered to this belief system we will never understand phenomena which operates outside of these parameters. We must make a leap—not of faith, but of consciousness—landing, as social psychologist Donald Michael puts it, "with both feet firmly planted in mid-air." This may seem like a precarious position, but from there we can have a new level of perception, which may include information from dreams, intution, altered states, strange lights in a night sky and aliens from other galaxies.

The Truth is Just Around The Corner

THE LANDSCAPE OF UFOLOGY CHANGES CONTINUALLY. MASS SIGHTINGS EBB AND FLOW. Government leaks and disinformation enhance, then obscure the terrain. My own disbelief in the weirder aspects of UFOs has been persistently challenged by the haunting sincerity of people with incredible stories to tell. I have been lured onward in this enthralling, yet frustrating, journey with the promise that the truth is just around the next corner.

There always seems to be a rumor that the government is about to release vital information or that a certain researcher has found the "smoking gun" which will prove—once and for all—the existence of UFOs. At one time I even thought that if I did enough hypnotic regressions with UFO experiencers I might even find the secret. Now I know better.

Inconclusively...

EACH TIDBIT OF INFORMATION RAISES MORE QUESTIONS THAN IT ANSWERS. Always there is something inconclusive: the witness is credible but there's no evidence, or there is an artifact but it is lost, or the analysis can be interpreted in conflicting ways, or proper funding is lacking so expensive scientific procedures can't be performed, or there's a film or photograph but it *could* have been faked. The better we get at detecting fakes, the better the technology becomes for creating them. There is always just enough information to spur on believers but never enough to convince skeptics.

Seeing is Believing

I'VE COME TO THE CONCLUSION THAT, WHILE SCIENTIFIC INQUIRY IS DEFINITELY IMPORTANT and must be continued, it is only through our individual experience that UFOs can be accepted. All the scientific data in the world will not convince a skeptic who doesn't believe. Yet one personal UFO sighting will do so.

My awareness of UFOs started with a dream and grew through sessions with believable people who talked about unbelievable experiences; meetings with researchers who had done exhaustive investigations; viewing films and photographs that did not seem faked; and seeing a star "fall" *up* during a UFO skywatch.

Yet to Come...

MY EXPERIENCE IS NOT OFFERED AS PROOF. I realize how "flakey" this sounds and how easily it is dimissed by those who haven't "done their homework" in studying the field. My journey through the labyrinth of ufology has convinced me something very real and very strange is going on, that cannot be eclipsed by hoaxes and hype. When the relentless ambiguities surrounding UFOs get to be too much, or the human squabbles that plague the UFO community make me want to flee, the universe presents a new surprise, sparkling with intrigue while whispering, "the most exciting part is yet to come."

Keep your eyes to the skies...

Dr. Virginia Bennett

VIRGINIA BENNETT HAS A PH.D. IN CLINICAL PSYCHOLOGY and is certified as a clinical hypnotherapist with a private practice in Berkeley, California. As a registered psychologist, Virginia also directs a program for the persistently mentally disabled at a community mental health center, teaches counseling psychology and provides training in hypnotherapy. Virginia is an investigator for the Office of Paranormal Investigations, sits on the Board of Directors of the International UFO Congress, and a member of the California Society for Psychical Study.

Virginia's life-long interest in research and clinical work in paranormal phenomena led her to examine—personally and professionally—past lives, mediumship, dreams, hauntings, out-of-body experiences, and psi, including training in remote viewing. She has made an extensive study of the field of ufology and uses hypnosis with people reporting close encounters with UFOs. Virginia's specialty is the exploration of altered states of consciousness and how personal psychology and paranormal events impact each other. In other words, Virginia Bennett wants to know: how *weird* can it get—and what does it all *mean*? www.HypnoGalaxy.com.

William Louis McDonald

ALIEN-UFO-ROSWELL ARTIST, INVESTIGATOR & LECTURER

BILL MCDONALD IS A FORENSIC ARTIST AND ILLUSTRATOR who is well known in the highly competitive field of UFO artistry. His illustrations, which include eleven different species of aliens from eye witness accounts and over twenty-five popular UFO disc and trianguloid spacecraft sightings, have been televised on "*Sighting*," "*Encounters*," "*Strange Universe*," and featured in *UFOs: A Manual For The Millennium*, and the book *Beyond Roswell*. Bill was the concept designer for the Showtime movie, *Roswell*, and *Gemini Encounters The Movie*, and has authored and illustrated articles for *Sci-Fi and Fantasy Models International, Fortean Times, UFO Magazine, MUFON International UFO Journal* and was the forensic artist behind two Testor Corporation model Kits of the "*Roswell UFO*" and the "*Crash Site*," with design assistance of the legendary John Andrews who was the Special Projects Chief Designer for the Testor Corporation.

Bill provides slide-show/lectures on the history of UFO cases, including Roswell, and cases involving eleven different alien species. He uses detective methods and standards in evidence collection that he used as an undercover private investigator for over fourteen years. He has documented testimonies from indepth interviews with military and civilian pilots, and science professionals.

The Alien/UFO/Roswell Art Online Gallery found at AlienUFOart.com, which displays detailed, high quality pen & ink illustrations from real alien/ UFO abductions cases. Bill can be reached by email at argonaut-greywolf@cox.net.

Ronin Books for Independent Minds

CHAOS AND CYBER CULTURE .... Timothy Leary $29.95 ___
    Cyberpunk manifesto on designing chaos and fashioning personal disorders (Out-of-print rare book)

ILLUMINATI PAPERS .... Robert Anton Wilson $14.95 ___
    Secret conspiracy of Sirius, the dog star. Wilson at his finest!

CROP CIRCLES .... Carolyn North $8.95 ___
    Fascinating introduction, filled with photos and diagrams by leading croppies

RIGHT WHERE YOU ARE SITTING NOW .... Robert Anton Wilson $14.95 ___
    Wilson teases your head inside out. Is it a conspiracy?

MUSINGS ON HUMAN METAMORPHOSES .... Timothy Leary $11.95 ___
    Were DNA seeds planted throughout the universe? Leary tells why it's nearly time to migrate - up!

LIVE CHEAPLY WITH STYLE .... Chick Callenbach $13.95 ___
    Smart ways to live better and spend less while caring for planet Earth

THE SCIENTIST .... John C. Lilly $14.95 ___
    Conversations with controller beings, how to use the void tank, talking to dolphins

WAY OF THE RONIN .... Docpotter $13.95 ___
    Riding the waves of change at work, cyberpunk career strategies

TURN ON TUNE IN DROP OUT .... Timothy Leary $14.95 ___
    How to start your own religion, Timothy as zen "trickster"

Check/MO payable to **Ronin Publishing,** mail to **POB 22900, Oakland, CA 94609**   **Books prices: SUBTOTAL** $_____

MC _ Visa _   Exp date _ _ / _ _ card #: _ _ _ _ _ _ _ _ _ _ _ (sign) _ _ _ _ _ _ _ _ _   CA customers add sales tax 8.25% _____

Name_   **BASIC SHIPPING: (All orders)**   **$5.00**

Address _ _ _ _ _ _ _ _ _ _ _ _ _ _ _ _ _ _ City _ _ _ _ _ _ _ _ _ State _ _ _ ZIP _ _ _ _ _   **PLUS per book SHIPPING**

Ph: 800/858-2665 • www.roninpub.com for online catalog   USA+$1/bk, Canada+$2/bk, Europe+$6/bk, Pacific+$8/bk _____
    price & availability subject to change without notice   **Books + Tax + Basic shipping + Shipping per book: TOTAL $**_____

Keep your eyes to the skies . . . .